12

SUN COUNTRY
COUNTRY
STYLE

SUN COUNTRY STYLE

PATRICIA HART McMILLAN &

KATHARINE KAYE McMILLAN

GIBBS·SMITH
P
PUBLISHER

SALT LAKE CITY

Title page: An accessories-filled niche is capped by a heroically scaled shell motif that brings a sense of countryside and seashore together in this sunny dining room.

Dedication page: Milling Road's mahogany huntboard, inspired by a colonial West Indies original, brings a sense of sun-loving tropics into any room.

Contents page: Interior designer Susan Zises Green added a sense of fantasy and fun to a sitting room in her Nantucket cottage with an overscaled border that is both sophisticated and naïve.

Text copyright © 1999 by Patricia Hart McMillan
and Katharine Kaye McMillan
Photographs copyright © 1999 as noted on page 144

First edition

02 01 00 99 4 3 2 1

Published by
Gibbs Smith, Publisher
P.O. Box 667
Layton, UT 84041
Orders (1-800) 748-5439
Visit our Web site at www.gibbs-smith.com

Designed by Traci O'Very Covey
Edited by Gail Yngve

Printed and bound in Hong Kong

Library of Congress Cataloging-in-Publication Data

McMillan, Patricia Hart.
    Sun country style / Patricia Hart McMillan and Katharine Kaye
  McMillan.
       p.   cm.
    ISBN 0-87905-910-9
    1. Country homes—United States—Decoration. 2. Interior
decoration—United States.   I. McMillan, Katharine Kaye.
II. Title.
NK2002.M42 1999
747.213—DC21   99–25658
                                            CIP

TO THREE REMARKABLE WOMEN

EVAN FRANCES AGNEW ❧ legendary home-furnishings editor, wonderful boss, dear family friend, and marvelous mentor who did her best to transform an ugly duckling into an editorial swan

ROSE BENNETT GILBERT ❧ noted home-furnishings editor, author, syndicated columnist, excellent boss, and great good friend who is the delightful coauthor of our *Decorating Country Style*, the first book on America's new country-style decorating trend

FLORENCE LATEZKI EPHLIN ❧ my aunt, who took the girl out of the country

CONTENTS

ACKNOWLEGMENTS
viii

FOREWORD
ix

INTRODUCTION
11

SEEKING THE SUN
17

ALL THROUGH THE HOUSE
27

SUN COUNTRY COLOR
49

ROOM BY ROOM
67

WINDOWS ON SUN COUNTRY
105

LIGHTING UP THE COUNTRY NIGHT
119

SUN COUNTRY ACCENTS
129

RESOURCES
140

PHOTOGRAPHIC CREDITS
144

ACKNOWLEDGMENTS

Authors get the lion's share of the glory of any book, but actually it is a small army of dedicated people working together in harmony who create any book. Here are those who contributed significantly to *Sun Country Style*:

First, credit goes to talented editor Gail Yngve, who shared my enthusiasm for this new design direction and placed her editorial expertise fully behind this project, and to Traci O'Very Covey, who designed *Sun Country Style*; she brought her exceptional design skills to creating an image that perfectly represents the subject matter.

Credit also goes to the photographers responsible for the incredibly beautiful images used in *Sun Country Style*. My deepest thanks belong to longtime professional and family friend Scott Frances. I also want to thank Robert Brandtley, Steven Brooks, Carlos Domonech, Andreas von Einsiedel, Emily Minton, John Nasta, Erik A. Roth, Jeremy Samuelson, Michael Skott, Bernard Tan, Steve Vierra, Peter Vitale, Dominique Vorillon, and Larry Watkins. Those whose work we published but whose names we failed to credit, please forgive us and accept our gratitude.

I want to express my special thanks to Charles Belleza, chief executive officer of Raphael Legacy Designs, who shared our enthusiasm and set about at once to create an exciting Sun Country Style Collection of furniture; to interior designer Joselito Dorotheo, who created exclusive room settings showcasing the furniture; to Lemuel Antonio Alegado, who provided research and development support; and to Albert Arriba, who made his home in the Philippines available for exclusive photography for the book.

To Norma Andrews, who made her vacation home available so that my ailing mother might recuperate there while I worked on the book. To Jane Cornell, noted home-furnishings author, who offered encouragement from her own sickbed. To Chris Casson Madden, hostess of HGTV's *Interiors by Design*, who was enthusiastic and supportive. To furnishings designer Raymond Waites, noted for his vintage style and for the design of his own American country-style book, for sending a photograph of his Hamptons living room to use in the book.

Hearty thanks to all who sent photographs and information: Denise Ladner, American Olean; Tom Lindell, American Standard; Linda Jennings, representative of American Standard who always responds with efficiency and grace to all editorial crises and demands; Linda Neal of Armstrong and Kelly Saccomanno of the Al Paul Lefton Company, who represent Armstrong; Jenny Hildreth of Sheila Fitzjones Public Relations in London, who supplied material from Amdega; Anita Riley of the Tile Promotion Board; Jason Burnett of *Southern Accents*; Jean-Paul and Ava Blachere of the Blachere Group; Anne Kelly, managing editor of *England's Country Homes and Interiors*; Donald McKay, director of sales and marketing for the Budji Collections; Linda Clas of William B. Johns & Partners, United States public relations representatives of Budji; Odile Servent, representative of Elitis; Sara Reep and Jodi Johnson of Fieldstone; Sergio Debbi of Florim Ceramiche; Frances L. Giknis, Georgia-Pacific; Ann Flower, representative of Guess Home Collection; Valerie Moran and Kim Huebner of Grange, USA; Tommy Boatwright and Jane B. Cummings, Sheffield & Galloway/Goodwin Weavers; Susan Zises Green's office staff; Sabrina Murphy of Eric Roth's office; Lisa Morrice for Houles-U.S.A.; Suzanne Pruitt for Habersham; Sarah P. Fletcher for Hunter Douglas; Jacqueline Greaves and Christine Abbate for the Italian Trade Commission's Ceramic Tile Department; Carrie Draves of the Kohler Company for Baker's Milling Road and Joyce Black of Rhombus Design Group for Milling Road; Lis King for Blonder Wallcoverings and Rutt Custom Cabinetry; Holly Krueger, Lexington Furniture Ind.; Bill Mitchell, the Mitchell Group; Faith Benson of Ronnie's Ceramic Company; Kelly Chandeysson of Rosemary Beach Land Company; Judith Smith of Reynolda House; Janis Clapoff and Sue Young of San Ysidro Ranch; Andrea Wasiak of L. C. Williams & Associates for Sauder; Frederic de Bernard, representing Salon de Meuble du Paris; Maurizio Placuzzi for SICIS; Robin Campbell, Stanley Furniture Company; Christine Demery of Souleiado; Serge and Stefani de Laville of Toujours Provence, importers of Souleiado and DeTonge; Adam Ash of White House Advertising for Textillery; Laurie Bailey of This End Up Furniture Company; Karen McNeill Harris, public relations representative for This End Up Furniture Company; Hillary K. Holland, Winterthur; Anne Martin and Debra Caserta, Westpoint Stevens, and to Joseph Grange, whose foreword succinctly expresses the *raison d'être* for *Sun Country Style*.

FOREWORD

Country and sun—these two words are magic for all our contemporary city dwellers living in crowded metropolises, whether they be in Europe, America, or Japan.

Country and sun are also a symbol of Mediterranean culture—that from which our civilization originates.

Living in the south of France, I have always had this dream to create the ideal home where the architecture is perfectly integrated into the landscape that surrounds it. Where everything is conceived to play with the light, whether it be to tame it in a shaded patio or to shield oneself from its rays by shuttered windows.

This game of hide-and-seek between light and home perhaps achieves its most beautiful balance in the marvelous countryside of Provence. The same game continues in Tuscany, in Andalusia, from Greece to Morocco, and finds itself transformed in Mexico.

It is this very chemistry that is explored in Pat McMillan's very beautiful book, illustrating just how this age-old tradition still inspires contemporary decoration and design today.

—Joseph Grange, Director
Groupe Grange

Every house has its dialect and customs. Different specialties and unique wine—from those houses with vineyards to produce them—create what the French call *"coleur locale,"* the color of life made more vivid by furniture imbued with *art de vivre,* or authenticity.

INTRODUCTION

here *is* something new under the sun—*Sun Country Style*. Wherever and whenever one finds the essential natural elements—warm sun, crisp air, soothing views—sun-country style can be found. Places where I have discovered the style range from Big Sur to Provence to Manila. Around the globe, a wholehearted celebration of sun's warming rays and

Cozy charm says country but lively colors and bold pattern say "sun country" in designer Susan Zises Green's Nantucket living room.

nature's enriching beauty has as its inspiration spring and summer sun, sky, and water. Light-filled, color-washed, and clean-lined, this new style graciously brings the sunshine and country inside our homes. This new, lighter, brighter contemporary mood with its sense of easy luxury and relaxed informality is a whole new living style that marries the charm of nature with the convenience of modernity.

In the United States, this new style is a far cry from Early American country-style rooms and its dark woods and harvest-inspired, earthbound color palette. The old country style—cluttered with collect-ibles and blanketed in drying herbs—is much too rooted in a musty past to move free-spiritedly into the future. No wonder that lovers of country style across the United States and around the world are doing what comes naturally. They are keeping the best—country's relaxed look—and changing the rest. By moving towards the lighter, brighter, more contemporary look, one might say that country style is singing a whole new song—one more in tune with the needs of the new millennium.

Perhaps the first clue to sun-country style is that these interiors wholeheartedly cele-brate the sun and natural light. Regardless of the cli-mate or architectural style, entire walls of efficient, high-tech glass flood rooms with natural light while holding cold or heat at bay. Wherever and whenever there are soothing views but not a lot of sunlight, a sunny color palette—based on the spring and summer sun, sky, and water—simulates the sun.

New rooms express a profound joy in and participate with the out-of-doors. They do this not merely with great walls of windows that open to miles of views but with doors that open wide onto porches, decks, terraces, patios, and loggias. Often, these outdoor rooms are re-plete with sit-a-spell rocking chairs, old-fashioned porch swings, and hammocks.

New sun-country rooms are clutter-free and casual.

Walls of windows with Gothic arches in this country-casual garden room make perfectly clear all the charms of the garden year-round.

There's a noticeably lighthearted and contemporary mood. Gone are many of the familiar American country elements based on Early American farmhouse decor. For example, one won't see now-cliché stacks of baskets and wooden watermelons. Gone, too, are strong references to chintz-filled English manor houses. Fabrics and furniture that are more today than yesteryear have replaced these familiar things.

Painted furniture—chipped and peeling or not—remains a part of sun country. But even fancifully decorated pieces are more practically designed with contemporary function in mind. Growing more popular than pretty painted feminine furniture are more masculine wood pieces in not-too-rich, not-dark natural finishes. Simplified designs based on traditional forms avoid type-casting. Versatile and easy to mix and match, they permit quick switches as seasons change and personal style grows.

The sun-country style, like its many predecessors, is im-bued with practical country sensibility but exhibits new per-sonal expression. For example, even exterior walls—like the occasional handmade quilt—might show up in an unex-pected pastel.

America's original coun-try style sneaked up on us as a part of our decorating heri-tage, and it has never entirely gone out of style. In 1975, while researching America's decorating past for a maga-zine series commemorating the Bicentennial that I was writing for *1,001 Decorating Ideas* (later *1,001 Home Ideas*), I was delighted to discover that a quiet decorating "revolution" had taken place. Perhaps it was more an evo-lution. At any rate, Early American style had given way to what had to be described as a brand new style.

Excited at having discovered a uniquely American decorating style, I discussed how to create a book about it with my former boss, Rose Bennett Gilbert, who had been editor-in-chief of *1,001 Decorating Ideas*. We

The next best thing to a hammock out-of-doors is one indoors,
like this one on an enclosed porch with a view.

proposed a book about the new style with art historian and editor Jean Anne Vincent at Doubleday, who enthusiastically urged us to write the book *Decorating Country Style*, published by Doubleday in 1979, which became the first book to define the new American country style.

This fresh look in decorating caught the fancy of many design writers. We soon discovered that we weren't the only ones to notice this look. *Decorating Country Style* was quickly followed by a plethora of books and magazines on the same subject. Soon, decorating magazine articles began to preach to readers that country was a mood, not a place; a lifestyle, not merely a decorating style. I had grown up on a Missouri farm, so while I could easily agree that a city dweller could decorate country style, I couldn't quite concede that decorating a New York City apartment country style and working as a New York City decorating magazine editor was creating a country lifestyle.

To me, it was enough that country was a decorating style that everyone everywhere could enjoy. Since the style dispenses with the artifice associated with formal historic styles, it's easy to achieve with or without the help of a professional decorator. But like all art, including folk arts and crafts, country-style decorating offered design challenges by calling for the creative use of fundamental aesthetic rules of design such as balance, rhythm, and harmony. No wonder it proved so appealing to decorating enthusiasts and amateur and professional designers alike. As the decorating editor of *1,001 Decorating Ideas*, one of the most widely read design magazines at the time, I was necessarily involved with all historic styles and periods. But I could decorate my own home and work with private clients to decorate their homes in their own personal expressions of country style.

Eventually, I left the city for Andrew Wyeth country in Pennsylvania. As concept director for the Franklin Mint's *Creative Home*, I worked with leading signature designers to create new home accessories and furnishings. Alas, none was interested in country.

My own view of country style was gradually changing. I wasn't fully aware that others, too, were quietly giving country a new look. It took awhile for me to realize that another quiet revolution or evolution was taking place. I have always loved country, but I sensed the need for an entirely new direction. In 1994, I helped to develop a design concept for a sunny country-style, Chippendale-inspired tall chest, crafted in wrought iron and wicker. The chest, created in the Philippines, made its debut at the International Furniture Center in High Point, North Carolina. It was warmly received. Even now, my partner

Rudy Santos and I continue to receive frequent inquiries about the country-style chest, which was the first hint that my own view of country style was changing. Such strong interest in this new version of country was a clue that it had dramatically reinvented itself.

In 1996, a career move back to full-time interior design brought me to the sunny South. As director of Office Design and Planning for a large New York City–based entertainment corporation, I was sent to Florida in 1996 to oversee the design of the company's new operations headquarters. After years in the Northeast, I was completely unprepared to experience such abundant daily sunshine and the incredible color palette that it inspired. To my surprise, I reveled in it. I began to notice that other designers such as Karin Blake of California, whose design for Candice Bergen's home appeared on the cover of *Architectural Digest*, were moving away from darker, traditional, woodsy country-style interiors into country-casual rooms as brightly colored as a summer garden on an August day. Some were even using more contemporary furniture, accessories, and fabrics.

By the next year, during a trip to the furniture and accessory shows in Paris, I saw clearly that English textile designers and other European designers had also discovered the south—France, Italy, and Spain. In response, they had created new lines of fabrics, wallcoverings, and accessories in rich, sun-inspired citrus colors with a distinct country-casual feeling. Vive la citrus! Vive la country! Although there were regional architectural and other influences, room settings designed to showcase their new products were not typical Provence, Tuscany, or Rivera interiors. Distinctly country in mood, they were beyond traditional regional country styles.

Shortly after that Paris trip, I began research for a new book, *Home Decorating for Dummies* (IDG, September 1998), with my daughter and coauthor, Katharine Kaye McMillan. We were thoroughly delighted to discover through interviews with interior designers across the United States that American country-style decorating had virtually moved to a very sunny south. After trips to the Philippines and China, the evidence was overwhelming. Designers around the globe were decorating in what could be considered a brand new country style—sun-country style.

As you will see here, sun-country-style rooms share a country-casual mood and a sun-loving, light-respecting color palette. Still, that leaves much room for differences of many sorts. There may be, for example, delightfully distinct geographic and cultural references. This is particularly noticeable when comparing interior designer Susan

Sun-country-style living spaces may be lively or serene—
dressed up or down. Anything goes, just as long as these
rooms are comfortable and relaxed.

Zises Green's Nantucket house, pages 6, 10, and 29; designer Budji's Philippines residence, pages 36 and 113; and both of those with the exciting and tropical St. Lucia house, pages 26, 37, and 38.

Historic decorating styles may also influence the new sun-country style. Among the interiors shown here are the traces of Early American, Arts and Crafts, French Provincial, and Scandinavian styles. Sometimes modern and traditional elements meet and mingle. Architect James Strasman's Vermont "Bridge House," pages 83, 88, 106, is an excellent example or the entirely contemporary California Big Sur house, pages 32–33.

Despite the many differences, the key sun-country-style element is that it encourages easy-going sunny interiors that have little to do with farms but everything to do with nature. It's a style that anyone can adopt anywhere in the world.

SEEKING
THE
SUN

eople have always sought the sun. Our continuing quest to bring more sunlight into homes and to open interiors to bigger and better views of the great outdoors has led to wonderful changes in architecture and interior design. Around the world, expansive large-paned windows, sweeping atriums,

Garden rooms—sometimes called "halfway" rooms because they seem midway between the house and garden—serve many functions, keeping nature always in plain sight.

vast skylights, and extensive sliding-glass doors all point to our passion for the sun.

As if breathtaking views and walls of windows were not enough, we also resort to the magic of color to simulate the presence of natural light when there is little. In places where sunlight is as precious as gold, brilliant color suffices for long spells of sunless time.

Wraparound porches, conservatories, Florida rooms, and garden rooms—delightful places in the sun—conjure images of endless summers in brilliant sunlight. The development of these architectural elements chronicle America's continuing flight from dark and gloomy colonial-era rooms with few, small, rudely glazed windows to ever-more innovative, light-filled spaces. Today, some of these historic places are resorts and museums, readily accessible to those who want to experience their charms firsthand.

Country homes in pastoral settings have a very long history. Even before the American Revolution, colonists were building country homes along riverbanks far from metropolitan centers. Although most early country houses were only one-story, modest log cabins, or Cape Cod–style homes, others were centerpieces of large estates, handsome structures in an English style. Some colonists, such as William Penn, imported skilled laborers to build both their town and country homes.

In the early days, it was thought good and proper for country houses to spread out (but not up) to better embrace the land. Thomas Jefferson took care that his one-and-a-half-story country home, Monticello, retained the look of a one-story structure. Much later, America's super wealthy built summer cottages in Newport that made no pretense at actually being cottages. Truth is, they were more mansions than cottages. Similar to Palladio's famed Italian villas, they were in the country, affording occupants opportunity to enjoy the beneficial effects of a cooler climate and nature, but they were not of the coun-

The soft gentle light of candles, protected from the wind by glass hurricane globes, makes lingering on the porch delightful long after the sun has gone down.

try. These magnificent cottages featured architectural and decorative styles we would consider formal today. No one particular cottage style dominated, and these structures were as varied as they were rich.

OLANA 🌞 However, none of the astounding Newport cottages has proven more interesting than Olana, the isolated country house that celebrated landscape artist Frederick Church built for himself in 1870. He built it atop an upstate New York hill overlooking the Hudson River. Loosely based on the exotic Persian style replete with towers, what Olana had in common with other American-country places was an array of porches and windows. These framed, extraordinarily dramatic, and beautiful views of the Hudson River and the surrounding countryside proved infinitely satisfying and inspirational to Church, whose large landscapes sometimes sold for tens of thousands of dollars.

The interior of Olana served as a unique canvas for Church's inventive interior decoration. Every surface was embellished with exotic patterns and colors that were both exciting and comforting.

REYNOLDA HOUSE 🌞 On the other hand, Reynolda House in Winston-Salem, North Carolina, was an expression of southern comfort. During the early part of the twentieth century in the American South, country living was the most desirable aesthetic environment. These country dwellers, many of whom were English transplants, fashioned their houses on English models, which were intended to serve as places in which to enjoy the out of doors. Here it was not fashionable to create immodestly monumental showplaces. Reynolda House is one of only a few early-twentieth-century American country houses still standing in almost its original form, according to Barbara Mayer, author of *Reynolda: A History of an American Country House.*

Designed by Charles Barton Keen, a Philadelphia

A space-saving "trundle" coffee table, designed by Patricia Hart McMillan with Raphael
Legacy Designs, sports a stone mosaic top that's practical and pretty. The table's
Chinese Chippendale motif mixes with traditionally dark furniture and modern seating
in this eclectic living room—a Philippines version of sun-country style.

Despite its large size, Reynolda House was deliberately
designed by owners Katharine and Richard Joshua Reynolds to
look like a bungalow nestled in the countryside, and that is
what they called it—The Bungalow.

architect, and built between 1912 and 1917, Reynolda
House boasts sixty-four rooms in 40,000 square feet.
Despite its size, the house was deliberately designed to
look like a bungalow. That's exactly what its owners, who
wanted their home to seem welcoming instead of intimi-
dating, called it—The Bungalow.

The vision of Katharine Reynolds, wife of tobacco
baron Richard Joshua Reynolds, founder of the R. J.
Reynolds Tobacco Company, Reynolda House was the
centerpiece of the 1,067-acre estate; a real working farm
surrounded it. Architecturally, the house was unique.
Instead of having a typical back and a front that faced a
formal garden, Reynolda House had two fronts and was
sited so that the family could enjoy views of a rolling lawn
on one side and Lake Katharine on the other. Views were
accessible from the many small and large porches.
Because fresh air was considered essential to good health,
each second-floor bedroom had its own adjoining sleeping porch. The large and lovely semicircular lake porch
was furnished with comfortable wicker furniture and was
a real country living room. Now glassed in, it is an early
example of what we call a garden room today.

Reynolda House interiors left the Early American
farmhouse light-years behind. Although interiors were
intended for informal living, they are much dressier than
today's relaxed country styles. Still, this important place
is now a museum that stands as a testament to America's
love for country living in a distinctly country style.

SAN YSIDRO RANCH ✣ San
Ysidro Ranch, in the foothills of the Santa Ynez
Mountains near Santa Barbara, California, is one of the
West Coast's earliest and most desirable country places.
The ranch has a long and colorful history quite different
from any country place on the East Coast.

Originally it was a way station for Franciscan padres
who were building a chain of missions along the road
from San Diego to San Francisco. In 1766, Spain's King
Carlos III granted title of the property to the Catholic
Church. It became a farm, supporting the nearby Mission
Santa Barbara and a contingent of soldiers at El Presido
Real, the fort that protected the mission. In 1822, Spain
ceded the area to Mexico. Three years later, Senor
Thomas Olivera, son of one of the original soldiers at

El Presido Real (now downtown Santa Barbara), married a woman from San Diego and built an adobe cottage at San Ysidro in 1825 that still stands and is used today as a private dining room.

After the ranch was granted to the United States in 1848, a series of settlers laid claim to it until Colonel Bradbury True Dinsmore of Anson, Maine, became the first Yankee to own the ranch. San Ysidro became home to his family and earned fame for its citrus, dwarf bananas, strawberries, sweet potatoes, and other fruits and vegetables grown there.

In 1935, the ranch, which had changed hands several times, became the property of hotelier and politician Alvin Carl Weingand and his partner, movie star Ronald Coleman. These two imparted star power to the ranch, turning it into the preferred place in the country for movie stars, politicians, socialites, and celebrities.

At San Ysidro Ranch, even the rich and famous could do all the things ordinary people were supposed to do in the country. They could revel in the unspoiled natural beauty and abundant sunshine of the perfect getaway place. They could enjoy the freedom of informality. They could totally relax in the unpretentious but charming main house and cottages whose porches provide breathtaking views of the nearby Santa Ynez Mountains and the Pacific Ocean. John and Jacqueline Kennedy stayed at San Ysidro Ranch during their 1953 honeymoon. The cottage where they stayed has been called Kennedy Cottage ever since.

In 1997, San Ysidro Ranch was redecorated. Designer Ron Hefler restored the ranch's vintage flavor, some of which had been lost during earlier remodelings. His careful designs preserve the sense of history that guests encounter upon entering the main gate. He thoughtfully retained the sense of "retreat rather than resort," as he brought interiors up to date and ready for the next decade.

Color, which is what sun-country style is largely about, extends to the outsides of houses that may sport pale and pleasing or plainly passionate pastels.

The newly decorated informal interiors blend the best of European and American country-house sensibilities, combining dignity with comfort. A medley of traditional patterned fabrics—large-scale florals, traditional checks, and country stripes—in bright warm colors that play against light walls and ceilings, lend cheer and charm.

San Ysidro Ranch—an outstanding example of America's early and continuing love of the sun and the country—is well prepared to enter into the next millennium, a continuing legend that looks both backward and forward to country living.

CONTINUING THE COUNTRY HOUSE TRADITION TODAY ❧ While Reynolda House and San Ysidro Ranch are links to our sun-seeking past, architects and designers today further the country-house tradition in a number of new ways. The technique that best blends past and present even as it anticipates the future is that of interpreting old forms in contemporary ways. An outstanding example is a Vermont country house by Toronto architect James Strasman. Based on New England's covered bridges, this structure is at the same time traditional and modern. Inside, ancient natural materials—wood, slate, stone—recall such early shelters as caves and groves, while a very modern building material—glass—is employed to protect even as it exposes the interior and its occupants to boundless light and endless views.

Elsewhere in this book, it will be easy to see regional architectural and interior design influences on sun-country style. However, what makes this new country style global in scope is not form, but substance. Sun-country interiors around the world share a common clarity of purpose—to celebrate the sun—that results in dignified, informal, and, therefore, country interiors that reflect the present and optimistically anticipate a bright and shining future.

Even bedrooms in sun country may have fireplaces! This one in the Kennedy Cottage—
so called because John and Jacqueline Kennedy spent part of their honeymoon
there—is at San Ysidro, an early example of sun-country style in California.

The living room in the Kennedy Cottage at San Ysidro blends design influences from
many different times, places, and cultures so that a sense of history mixes with a sense
of anticipation of a bright and cheerful future—a true sun-country decorating spirit.

What could be more country than a porch like this one on which to dine casually or rock away the cares of the day, surrounded by the bliss of a beautiful garden? Bright white chairs with bentwood backs surround a wicker table set with refreshments.

Country kitchens are synonymous with all the comforts of home. Opting for greater serenity and peace of mind, new country-style kitchens keep clutter under control and collections to a minimum.

ALL
THROUGH THE
HOUSE

Historic styles and periods spring from specific times and places. They're easy to identify and describe. Today, design movements are apt to spring up at any number of places around the world, the result of a universal mood swing. It's not always a quick or easy process to

This island living room goes its own way, passing up pattern in favor of plain peaceful surfaces, leaving behind all references to the English manor houses and their chintz-covered couches or to New England farmhouses filled with patchwork quilts.

identify and describe a new decorating style, particularly when there are variations. Sun-country style is the result of a global decorating movement that seeks and celebrates the light. It's an almost reflexive response to an irrepressible desire to bring more of the beneficial rays of sunshine indoors, to make the most of outdoor living possibilities. The elements—furniture, fabrics, accessories—vary from place to place, country to country; but the sun-country design objective—to celebrate the light and nature, indoors and out—remains the same. It's just achieved in different ways in different places.

Creature comforts—physical and emotional—are at the heart of all country decorating, and that's especially true of this style. Furniture is built and arranged for relaxation. Convenience places the focus on the inhabitants, not the habitat, for home is not an object, nor is elaborate decorating an objective. Shock is out. Serenity is in. Clutter, an endearing element in other country styles, is rejected.

Sun-country style may enjoy the same goals everywhere it is found, but individualism is essential. A simple reason is that what some find comfortable and comforting, others may not. There's also the genuine satisfaction that comes from putting our personal stamp on our own home. This imbues it with real meaning, reinforcing the fact that we matter. Individualism makes our homes sacred, set apart—our own special refuge or haven, a vital need today.

Fortunately, with an abundance of affordable materials at our disposal, individualism has never been easier to achieve. Sun-country style does not restrict anyone to a brief menu of limited choices. The style's simple objectives and principles allow great freedom of expression in unique ways. A look at homes across the United States and around the world reveals truly creative, distinctly different approaches to this welcoming new international country style.

Decorating starts with the beautifully colored front door of designer Susan Zises Green's Nantucket home with its gem-box-sized front porch that turns aside from the street to welcome callers.

ACROSS THE NATION

NANTUCKET—MASTERING THE MIX   Susan Zises Green bought a gray shingle-covered cottage that on the outside is very similar to others in quaint and charming Nantucket. Inside, it's a world apart. The decorating vision realized, based on her ideas of what might once have been there, is all her own—a timeless cottage style based on English examples and filtered through the American experience. It's warm, inviting, graceful, and charming because, Green says, "It's a tough world. Most of us work, and we want to come home to a place that's welcoming."

Reminiscent of the past but very much of today, Green's Nantucket getaway is full of visual delights. Decorating began with furniture that Green, a leading New York City interior decorator, already owned—a great mix of pieces from here, there, and everywhere. There were Adirondack twig pieces acquired in Woodstock, a wicker table from the Philippines, a spool table from Tennessee, a nineteenth-century antique cabinet, furniture pieces found at garage sales and auctions, and an upholstered piece covered in its original twenty-year-old Lee-Jofa linen that still looks fresh.

"The furniture, from my former upstate New York house, looks entirely at home in Nantucket," says Green.

What was needed to get this mix together? Just the right color palette. Green began by painting and stenciling cold white entry walls in soft summery celadon green with earthy terra-cotta brown accents.

"I chose green because it's the most restful color on earth! It's calm, soothing, breezy, and yummy. I love it," she says. Living-room walls are a sunny pale yellow stria (a combing technique that layers colors in miniscule stringlike stripes). They're topped with a hand-stenciled black-and-cream border that adds unexpected punch.

The dining-room and kitchen walls were treated by a

An inviting sofa and sprightly chairs gather round a generous
table in a dining room with split-pea-soup-colored walls—
design by Susan Zises Green.

local artist to multi-coats of hand-sponged and dry-brushed
paints that end up looking like a delicious split-pea-soup
green.

"People marvel," says Green. Master-bedroom walls,
surprisingly covered in a collage of tramp-art-like corrugated cardboard that adds great texture, are painted a soft
gray. Stenciling adds more color and interesting pattern
to walls throughout but is most striking in the parlor,
where the fascinating stencil pattern is based on old pottery. Green included the name of the original builder and

owner of the house, along with names of her own family
members in the design.

The house is full of wonders, but "Nantucket is about
nature, about being outdoors," says Green. "I wanted the
light to come in, so I hung lace and sheer curtains. I enjoy
seeing the sky from indoors."

FLORIDA — CREATING A BRIGHT
HARBOR ⸙ Jack Fhillips had eyed the old shipbuilder's house by the sea for fifteen years. By the time he

Designer Jack Fhillips describes the chic simple and ever-so-casual blue, white, and khaki color scheme of his Palm Beach cottage as "very Brooks Brothers."

bought it, this popular Palm Beach interior designer and antiques dealer had ideas galore about how he wanted to update its considerable charm. Transforming it into a typical tropical beach house was not one of them. In fact, one would never suspect from looking at the finished interior that the cottage is only a few miles from toney Worth Avenue in Palm Beach, where Fhillips has his shop. There's not a tropical seashell in sight.

Essentially, Fhillips wanted to make his new haven lighter, brighter, and more cheerful. It was to be a tad more refined, but not serious. His new weekend getaway was to have the feeling of a playhouse—for grown-ups.

Fhillips began the cottage's transformation by giving

rooms a crisp white background. "It makes everything stand out," he says. By "everything," he means a medley of furnishings that are mostly an unpretentious mix of English and American styles in sturdy country oak. To show off the furniture and enhance its sculptural quality, he painted both walls and woodwork in some rooms white. In some areas, floors are also white. In those instances, new pine floors were treated to a whitewash finish, a colonial New England technique that looks surprisingly sophisticated and current.

Walls in other rooms are treated to a light-and-lively blue-and-white-striped wallpaper, a basis for the blue-and-white color scheme throughout the house that calms and cools Florida's tropical heat waves. Blue-and-white stripes show up not just in wallpaper, but also in slipcovers, lamp shades, and draperies to create just the right amount of low-key pattern play and excitement.

What could be more nautical or nicer with that white background and oak furniture than a chic, simple, blue-and-white scheme? Actually, for greatest interest, there's a range of blues—from navy to sky to marine—in fabrics used for slipcovers, draperies, and the occasional antique quilt.

"Very Brooks Brothers," is the way Fhillips describes the blue-and-white scheme that gets a discreet color boost from touches of khaki and nautical flags in bright red and yellow. It's accurate to say that his is a very personal color scheme: "I live in blue, khaki, and white," Fhillips says, meaning that those are the colors he wears. Proving that point and perhaps making another, Fhillips points to white toss pillows made from his cast-off cable-stitch sweaters.

Accessories are favorite collections of old sailing-ship paintings, blue-and-white pottery, and boat and fishing gear—presented in an orderly sun-country fashion.

Accessories may be functional or just about anything that adds visual interest, plays up a theme, and piques curiosity. In this instance, designer Jack Fhillps nonchalantly stands a bunch or worn paddles on end.

Fhillips admits that he has been startled by the enthusiastic response to his house since it appeared in *Veranda*, a national decorating magazine. "It's just a simple cottage," he states, almost quizzically, which is akin to saying that a diamond is just a stone.

SANTA FE—ACHIEVING WESTERN UNION ⚘ Traditional Santa Fe–style rooms with dark adobe walls, viga ceilings, and earthy quarry-tile floors are womb-like shelters for cluttered collections and indigenous art. Originally endearing but in danger of becoming a cliché, Santa Fe style is becoming cleaner, simpler . . . more sun country, a real western union of old and new.

Most noticeably, earth tones are giving way to earth

tints. Dark, cave-like color palettes are being traded for lighter, brighter backgrounds for living. Cool color choices range from cool grays and whites to beiges (which, if one isn't careful, can look too monochromatic and modern), or palest blues and greens. On the warm side of the color wheel, there's apricot, corals, or ochres (which, if not lightened up, can look too Provençal or Tuscan).

What moves Santa Fe style into sun country while maintaining its identity is its new balancing act; that is, rooms are not too regionally ethnic (fewer or no *santos* collections, little reference to southwestern textile art). They're not too devoted to antique architectural features; instead, strong architectural elements are often painted out to blend them in. Interiors are neither too formal nor too casual. Care is taken that the style remains country casual, but not too quaint or whimsical. And new homes, such as Carol Burnett's much-publicized house, introduce elements from beyond Santa Fe. Updated interiors are not too contemporary, even though there is some contemporary furniture and perhaps even some contemporary art.

Sun-country comfort may demand contemporary upholstery, but covers are country-casual linens or woven cottons. Furniture is apt to be updated in lighter finishes with only an occasional dark oak piece and a few painted pieces added to the mix.

When it comes to accessories, the emphasis is on fewer, more important pieces that form a new union between western and worldly treasures.

BIG SKY COUNTRY—CORRALLING A MOUNTAIN HIGH ⚘ Rita Kissner, a Houston, Texas, interior designer, chose local artisans and materials for a Montana house she designed for clients. For example, artisans Eric Rempp framed mirrors in found elk horns, Jeffrey Funk forged custom andirons and hinges, and Collin Leach crafted pine beds. But nothing about this lodgepole-pine house in Big Sky Country screams "Montana."

"The owners wanted a simple, practical home; and, while they wanted great style, they didn't necessarily want Montana style," says Kissner. There's not one hokey cowpoke reference. This house is anything but nouveau cowboy. On the contrary, there's something slightly Italian country and vaguely French Provincial about the design—probably the combining of wrought iron and stone boulders along with Souleiado fabrics, sans frills, from Provence in southern France. Then there are those Early American references: the punched-tin pie-safe panels in the kitchen cabinet fronts and rocking chairs all in a row on the big open porch. American country influences are felt in myriad ways, including the mix of contemporary upholstery with an assortment of wood furniture.

What gives this rustic home, with its dash-of-this-and-pinch-of-that approach, real sun-country panache is sophisticated simplicity, fresh as a cool mountain breeze on a hot summer day.

BIG SUR—MAKING A POINT ❧ Architect Mickey Meunning's design for Partington Point on California's Big Sur Coast is an engineering marvel that places the house, perched 275 feet above the Pacific Ocean, at the epicenter of constantly changing surrounding nature.

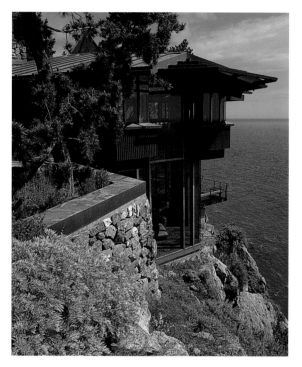

Living in Big Sur country means living on the edge, literally. Here, outdoor materials such as redwood, fieldstone, and slate move happily indoors.

Outside, heavy timbers and a skin of Cor-Ten metal—guaranteed to rust to just the right aesthetic—put this country house entirely at ease in its natural setting. Inside, walls of floor-to-ceiling glass create the sensation of being on a big front porch in the sky or in the cockpit of a high-performance jet plane or space shuttle, ready to lift off at a moment's notice. Panoramic views of ocean, sky, and the majestic mountainside from which the house seems to emerge are breathtaking.

Redwood beams, stone fireplaces, and slate terraces—materials chosen for weatherability—link the house securely with its environment. Leather-covered sofas, simple wood furniture, and subtly colored rugs call no attention to themselves but are in complete subjection to exterior views. Furnishings contribute to the sense of oneness of the house and nature. Partington Point in all points is an excellent example of California's heroic sun-country style.

AROUND THE WORLD

MEXICO ❧ Mexico's indigenous country style is notoriously exuberant and decidedly sun and fun loving. It draws on a variety of historic sources, including Roman, Moorish, and Spanish ancestry, a pre-Columbian past, and a brush with the French culture. Now, as more people from the north find second homes south of the border, there are discernible North American influences and sensibilities that have much to do with a sense of organization. New kitchens and bathrooms, for example, are likely to be bigger and more important. Surfaces such as walls, floors, and countertops in these new spaces wear newly made tiles in antique patterns.

Throughout, there are local cultural references; but seen through fresh eyes, they're handled with an appreciation that breathes new life into ancient forms. Transitional outdoor living areas such as loggias—sheltered from weather, fitted with fireplaces, and serenaded by nearby fountains—are key to Mexico's sun-country style. These spaces, furnished for lounging and dining, together with rooms open to the exterior, make the most of surrounding gardens and nature's soothing balm.

Furnishings from a variety of places and eras lend a cosmopolitan flavor to country-style rooms in Mexico. Indigenous Mexican country furniture, based on Spanish, French, and even Oriental styles, is widely diverse. But, sun-country style is not limited to the use of just

Sun-country-style living rooms, such as this Big Sur interior,
mix modern and contemporary elements with ancient natural
materials, beautifully blending and arranging them so that
nature is the focal point.

Michael Benasra's gaily decorated outdoor kitchen invites his
guests to dine al fresco, shielded by its tiled roof from the full
force of the California sun and occasional rain.

country-style furniture. There's apt to be a mixture of
plain and fancy, old and new furniture.

Here, as everywhere around the world, the emphasis
on gracious informality creates a distinct country mood.
That mood, which sometimes approaches playful
elegance, is enhanced by walls sponge-painted in sun-
dappled colors. Reportedly, some say that everyone in
Mexico is an artist-architect who cares deeply about the
color of a house. Painted and antiqued finishes for cabinetry and accent furniture, colorful native pottery, and
fabulously patterned native cotton fabrics all contribute
to a sensation of perpetual sunshine. It's a sunshine that
in the hands of architects like Mexico City's Ricardo
Legorreta, who mixes such dazzling palettes as ochre,
pink, and blue, asks to be touched, handled, tasted, and
made a veritable part of one's life. Ole!

E N G L A N D ☼ England is credited with
having invented the country-house style as Americans
know it. Americans realize that Palladio and others built
country villas in Italy, French aristocrats retired to their
chateaux, and even China's empress had her summer
palace. But we give the English all the credit for the idea
of the country-house-and-chintz style that Americans
continue to expand upon in their own casual image.
We're grateful for the country-house concept, but what
we're most thankful for at this point in history is the conservatory—the glass house that's predecessor to America's
garden-room craze.

Amdega, founded in 1874, is England's oldest conservatory company in continuous production. The
English grew orange and lemon trees in garden tubs during the summer, then moved trees and tubs into heated

conservatories before first frost. These glass houses, or "winter gardens," came into their own in the Victorian age, when people began to replace plants in conservatories, which they furnished as living spaces. Detached from the main house, conservatories were used for all manner of gatherings, including lovers' trysts. Today, the conservatory is more likely to be attached to the main house and called a sunroom. It is used for everything from a breakfast room to a home office. Some call these spaces "halfway houses"; that is, halfway between the house and the garden. Without these glass houses, outdoor living is risky business because of the vagaries of weather. With them, sun lovers can enjoy every last ray year-round.

Originally, interiors of English conservatories and garden rooms were white— but no longer. Now, any color goes along with the typical wicker and rattan and occasional Adirondack furniture from America.

Americans who latched onto the English country-house concept rose to the glass house hook, line, and sinker. First, they added windowed "Florida rooms." Now, the all-glass garden room in America has become as ubiquitous as the great room. Like the English, Americans use their glass houses (rooms) for everything under the sun—and the moon. When it comes to glass houses, no one's throwing stones. Glass rooms are helping both the English and Americans to lighten up . . . sun-country style.

Glass rooms, called garden or sunrooms, may be furnished like any other room—living, dining, lounging—only materials must be fade-proof and soft colors are kinder in intense bright light.

F R A N C E ❧ Provence in southern France is quintessential sun country. The area is world renown for two things: the unique quality of its light recorded by countless artists and its very natural, highly distinctive style. That style is bold, colorful, comfortable, readily available in materials well crafted by manufacturers who have become its legendary interpreters. Among them are DeTonge, a maker of beautifully painted furniture in traditional country designs, and Souleiado, creator of brightly colored, highly patterned cotton fabrics that are synonymous with the region. Purportedly, the name *Souleiado* is a Provençal word that means "the sun's rays shining through a cloud after a rain."

Recently, a fabric designer from England and an expatriate American designer now based in Paris, along with designers from other countries, have discovered Provence and let its style influence their own. Noticeably, they've borrowed its rich strong palette of colors such as ochre, olive, and cypress greens, sky and Mediterranean blues, passion red, and sunflower yellow. They and a new crop of French companies, such as Elitis, are incorporating the spirit of Provence into wall-coverings, fabrics, and accessories that are more contemporary in feeling, pulling the Provençal style into the orbit of the newer sun-country style.

P H I L I P P I N E S
❧ The Philippines are a vast number of South Seas islands inhabited by more than one-hundred ethnic tribes, many known for their extraordinary skills as craftsmen. The islands are home to amazing materials, including coral stone, used for steps and walkways; young marble stone, from which marvelous mosaics are made; and bamboo, used for constructing roofs, walls, and railings as well as beautiful furniture. There are rattan, cane, anahau palm (whose leaves line interior ceilings) and *abaca* and banana fibers, used for fabrics. These materials never take on artifice or lose their natural look. They keep the sense and wonder of nature always near, tying the user ever more closely to the out-of-doors.

Filipinos such as furniture and mosaic manufacturer Charles Belleza (head of Raphael Legacy Designs of Cebu in the south) and Budji (designer Antonio Layug's pet childhood name, now used professionally) in northern cosmopolitan Manila, enjoy a rich design heritage. That heritage includes influences from both Spain and China.

Add global travels to that rich mix, and it's easy to understand the cross-cultural elements that make their work appreciated worldwide.

Wherever Belleza travels around the world, his Filipino-made furniture of wrought iron and stone mosaic goes with him, taking along a little of that tropical country's magic and spreading its own sunshine. His meetings with heads of furniture companies and interior designers around the globe result in a mingling of ideas that bring new international styles to the fore.

Budji's career has led from personal style development and training, to interior design, to furniture design. He's credited with transforming lowly bamboo into the material of choice for chic furniture around the world. Increasingly, nature and the environment—the quality of winter light in Greece, the cool breezes of Tagaytay in the Philippines, with its white sand beaches—are central to Budji's designs. His country-house designs reflect his fascination with the mystical qualities of light, wonderful antiques, and primitive art. They work beautifully with his own contemporary furniture designs in a delightful mix that exemplifies the best in sun-country style in the Philippines.

CARIBBEAN ✤ In the old days, typical Western Hemisphere islands interiors would probably have featured furniture in England's East Indies style. Made of mahogany with cane inserts that let air circulate, designs were based on European models and simply blended into earth-tone backgrounds—but no longer.

Crisp, clean, light, and very bright color schemes announce the arrival of sun-country style in the Caribbean. If one is in search of a dramatic, foolproof color scheme, he or she can follow the example of a new house by a young English builder on St. Lucia—pure white throughout for walls, floors, ceilings, and furniture. At once

A simple linear chaise makes lounging a breeze on this terrace that's open to the soothing calm of the garden at the home of Filipino furniture designer Budji. Accessories are few but dramatic.

identified with the magical Greek Isles, it's a color that travels well from one sun-country island to another, even though they may be on opposite sides of the globe. Gorgeous in Greece, white is just as effective in the Caribbean, where it stands in stark and spectacular contrast to the brilliant blues of sky and water and the vibrant greens of lush foliage. Its very cleanness, like that of a white-sand beach, invites relaxed lounging during the midday heat and while a fiery sun sets across an endless bay. And its whiteness leaves memories of typically dark colonial Indies-style furniture that eventually made its way to these islands in a dim and distant past, making it blissfully easy to focus on the pleasures of the day.

When choosing white, one should choose easy-care heavy cotton fabrics for slipcovers and bedcovers that can be machine washed and slipped back on without ironing. Dark furniture should be given several coats of glossy white oil-base paint that can be quickly and effortlessly wiped clean. For added impact, choose deeply carved or excitingly woven wicker pieces with exotic ethnic origins. To match or not to match is not the question. Comfort is.

Flooring for a sun-country-style Caribbean house should be white nature stone, or color through porcelain ceramic tile, or painted floorboards. Whitewash or paint is the best choice for wooden walls and ceiling. Dark beams and heavy timbers can be transformed with fresh white paint to give island architecture a contemporary look that's young, playful, and vital.

For accents, any preferred color or colors can be chosen—one at a time, or altogether. Blue is a universal favorite with mythical appeal. Stefanidas blue, named for the famous Greek designer who's made it his signature, is a good bet. But one should feel free to choose his or her own signature color, one that makes a truly personal decorating statement.

Everything is whitewashed in this island living room that points to one important fact: casual, relaxed, and comfortable say country in any language around the globe.

A passel of pillows and banquette built beneath
a window cozy up to a table set for a snack.

This pristine white bedroom sparkles in the
slanting rays of the tropical St. Lucia sun.

In Mexico, a jewel-like sunburst arching against an ochre-colored wall creates a focal point for al fresco dining at a plaid-covered table surrounded by rustic chairs.

Corrugated paper is an unexpected and unique covering for the
walls of designer Susan Zises Green's Nantucket bedroom.
Sheer curtains let in the light, provide a measure of privacy,
and allow a peek at the outdoors.

Designer Rosemari Agostini's Dallas, Texas, garden-room loggia
is as abloom as a summer garden with flowers on chair fabric,
table, and china.

The classic double-hung window, topped with a graceful sheer blind,
lights the second-floor landing of designer Susan Zises Green's cottage.
Simply framed art adds color and makes passing this way a pleasure.

Simplicity and order give this Montana log cabin kitchen-dining area by
interior designer Rita Kissner its modern sun-country mood.

Traditional country cotton fabrics by Souleiado in France add
pleasant patterns to a sunny dining area. Colorful plates make
lively accessories for the built-in cabinet.

Kitchens, traditionally the heart of the home, get the lion's share of decorating attention in today's homes that glory in and play up the enduring appeal of natural materials, functional and attractive utensils, and enticing edibles.

Dining outdoors is de rigueur in the country, where a round table like this one in Provence is considered the most democratic—there is no head or foot—and convivial.

Valerie Moran of Grange Furniture says that even not-too-fussy traditional furniture can reflect the mood set by country-style backgrounds and accessories, like those in this French-country dining room.

SUN
COUNTRY
COLOR

Nothing feels more sun country than sparkling shades of color inspired by the abundant hues of beach, desert, meadow, and wood. Bold and brilliant, subtle and shy, casual and carefree—sun-country color palettes magically create moods that bring us instantly to these wondrous

Sunlight and shadow make colors by the sea mysterious and add to the sense of shelter on this porch in Seaside, Florida.

Colors for houses by the sea may take their color cues from
surrounding nature. Sheer white curtains go with any scheme,
filtering sunlight and softening colors.

places of nature. These palettes range from bleached pales
to deepened hues and from ethereal tints to passionate
tones. Color may be subtle and still as a pristine white or
strong and vibrant as tangy citrus. What all palettes have
in common is their luminosity. Brilliant light seems to
shine from within, not simply to reflect from the surface.
These confident colors just look and feel right.

Such extraordinary color as found in sun country
gives us a surge of emotion. The rainbows, dawns, and
sunsets of sunny climates have inspired poets and painters
for centuries. Now, they inspire those decorating in country style. Here is how leaders of the look are using the new
sunnier colors.

LAYERING ❧ Nature uses color freely
and widely, painting the ground beneath one's feet in
bold strokes of deep color, blending in accents and highlights all around us, and finally dusting the sky with a
sweep of blue and white. In this new country style, color

cues come from nature, which *layers* colors. In sun country, layering takes place in two ways. Colors may be layered on a particular surface such as a wall, or color
schemes may layer several colors within a room.

The look of many country surfaces often suggests layers of under and over pigments. No matter if a palette is
sheerest white or richest earth tints, the most arresting
colors are actually complex layers of glazes, tints, and
tones. In a sense, the effect of layering paint on a wall in
this way—especially in combed and other faux finishes—
looks similar to distressed, painted antique furniture.
Wear imperfectly reveals layers of paint that begin to look
impressionistic and mysterious. It is impossible to decide
just what color any color is precisely. Walls in designer
Susan Zises Green's Nantucket home are treated to layers
of paint in a stria, or combed, manner; and, as a result, she
says, when people see her dining-room walls, they are
amazed.

The simplest sun-country color palettes begin with

Bold patterns add even more punch to a bold color scheme. Textural interest plays up the lively mood begun by color and pattern play.

one wonderful color. That hue may be as pale and soft as morning mist or as bold and exciting as a handful of zinnias. Then that color is repeated and layered in its several tints and tones. This monochromatic, single-color idea is anything but monotonous, often elegant, always serene. It is an especially popular technique for faux-painted walls. But this approach also works beautifully for color scheming.

Some sun-country interiors layer two to three closely related hues to create an analogous color scheme. Warm oranges, yellows, and reds are a favorite scheme. These wow-powered citrus colors in lighter, slightly more contemporary versions of traditional Mediterranean ochre and yellow seem both familiar and fresh. This color

approach can be seen in faux-painted walls, patterned fabrics, furniture finishes, and interiors.

Complementary color stories for interior schemes often mix as many as five hues. Mastering this mix involves careful selection of proportions. Here, designers simply follow in nature's footsteps, using gentle neutral colors for large spaces, more intense ones for smaller areas. The brightest, boldest accent colors are used just as nature does—as small distinct accents.

CHOOSING A SUN COUNTRY PALETTE ❧ A wide range of choices makes choosing a palette that expresses one's personal point either extremely easy or very difficult. Those who know which color palette appeals to them will find it easy to choose, while those who find it difficult to choose between warm or cool sides of the color wheel, pale or passionate pastels, light or lively colors and more, will need time. Here are some options.

A super-cool color scheme guaranteed to bring the thermometer down a few notches is the misty green, turquoise, and particular deep blue palette seen in ocean waters surrounding Caribbean resorts. Layered on various surfaces and in furnishings for greatest contrast, these colors are romantic, restful, and exotic.

New country favorites are the whisper-soft colors that seem almost not to exist—the perfect pales. These irresistibly tender hues recall fragile summer blooms and delicate wisps of daybreak clouds. Glowing with an inner light, they hint at many things. The perfect pales change almost imperceptibly with the changing light to become virtually one shade, then another, and impossible to describe in simple standard phrases.

What makes these perfect pales so sun country is their remarkable but gentle vitality. More color than pristine white, perfect-pale tints impart a sensationally subtle hint of

Tied back as though they were draperies, cheerful gingham-checked shower curtains make the white, footed bathtub the star of this playful bath.

lively color that is pleasing and soothing. Softened shades of these pales complement but do not compete with furnishings, accessories, and scenic views.

Perfect pales can be tints and tones of a single multi-dimensional hue. Linen, an almost white, can deepen to flax, a stronger neutral. These nearly one-color schemes are the most subtle form of country color. What makes these elegant schemes still sunny is luminosity and complexity. They can also look glorious when two to three similar hues combine to enhance each other. Several tints of warm yet pale shades of yellow, orange, and cream are instant sun-country spring meadow. For a down-by-the-sea appeal, designers simply layer three shades of cooling greens and green-blues, ranging from sea foam to mist.

Another way pales are being layered is by playing off warm shades and cool tints in a complementary color scheme.

The passionate pastels bring a new vibrance to country interiors. Reminiscent of the riotous colors of a glorious flower garden in full bloom, these new upbeat country colors seem very here and now. They include the hot pinks, clear blues, brilliant yellows, and pastel purples of zinnias, morning glories, hibiscus, hanging fuschias, bearded iris, tulips, and more. Designers are unexpectedly pairing these strong colors with equally strong rustic-wood furniture.

On the opposite end of the spectrum, those who once loved earth tones are exchanging the darker tones for newer tints. Look for these new neutrals in colors that speak of white sand, sun-bleached grasses, faded adobe, and weathered shingles. Imagine them as layered tints with extraordinary patinas that add richness to ordinary surfaces.

The rich earthy ochre oranges, odd yellow-golds, and all their in-between permutations seen in traditional French and Italian country houses are showing up now in slightly lighter, somewhat dustier versions. It's easy to think of these soft pumpkins, rich corals, and gray- and green-golds as old-country colors, but they're really new-world inventions.

The color palette for country mountain homes, however, is influenced by tall trees, greenery, and moss. Imagine even bright colors made to appear just a little dusty and less relentlessly upbeat—more relaxed. These colors create an immediate sensation of coolness and even dimness so that by comparison sunlight seems brighter. One designer pits these mountain colors with soft whitewashed surfaces that provide interesting contrast without being jarring. Another designer paints wood surfaces the color of Spanish moss because it is calming.

Though sun country is about color, it also includes vibrant white—pure and simple or layered and complex.

This sun-country dining room was created by placing the family dining table catercorner to the crisp white fireplace and setting it with casual woven place mats. A floral rug, exuding a flower-garden feeling, completes the room.

In reality, white is a marvelous reflection of the brilliance of light and is the absence of color. While nature effortlessly produces countless shades and tints of white, an enormous amount of ingenuity by paint companies was needed to re-create these values. In nature and in synthetic products, white encompasses thousands of barely there whispers of tints and tones from snow to eggshell, linen, and more.

As a country color statement, white seems clean, current, and striking in its simplicity. White piqué, linen, lace, muslin, wicker, sand, stone, painted clapboard, and porch posts all conjure images of pure, innocent, simple summer.

The first all-white room was dazzling in its freshness. Legendary designer Sister Parish reminded us of that when she painted a motley collection of furnishings white for her Maine getaway. With all its freedom and informality, white lends a cool airiness and a certain nonchalance to any space. It effortlessly sets off the brilliance of views from windows, skylights, and open doors. Elegant and clean, it forms the ideal backdrop for the vivid colors of meadow and sky or ocean and sky. Juxtaposed with such lush surroundings as those of the St. Lucia and Jack Fhillips houses, white continues to surprise.

Selecting the perfect white for country homes as

Dressed up in a mix of gaily colored floral fabrics and country-
fresh gingham checks and plaids, a window seat becomes a
cozy reading corner in a living room.

It is not necessary to paint simple wooden furniture to make it more compatible with today's country. Give it a lift with light-and-lively wallcoverings and light colored cushions.

different as the one in St. Lucia and Fhillips's Florida house is actually complicated, requiring a great deal of finesse. Differences in natural light and each home's location along with the various times of day must be considered. Generally, cool whites look best in morning light; warm whites are more compatible in afternoon light.

"I like yellow white," says Phillips. "It's softer, creamier. It makes people look good. Gray whites are cold and make a funny cast on one's skin. I hate pinky whites, which throw funny shadows, and I use it only as an accent. When a pink-white is used, one absolutely *must* use some red with it!"

An up-to-date interior often combines two or more distinct shades of white and a variety of richly interesting (not necessarily expensive) textures. Walls might be linen white (which has a hint of yellow) and woodwork a zinc white, with upholstery in natural white linen and draperies in a novelty-weave cotton, linen, or flax in a bone or oyster color. The all-white room is kept intriguing by adding details and accessories.

Whatever the color palette, sun-country interiors all have a sparkling, sun-kissed appeal. Unexpected and innovative, they move beyond traditional country palettes, incorporating richer and usually more vivid hues. The effect is one of blending the out-of-doors with the in—bringing the sun and nature inside.

One way to wake up to sunshine and a view is to place a bed
near—perhaps in front of—a French door or window.

Simplicity, a hallmark of the new country mood, does not mean forsaking traditional country-style furniture, so long as it's surrounded with light colored walls and floor covering.

Painted furniture, especially white finishes, plays up sunny color schemes, adds a sense of freshness, and keeps small-scale rooms looking larger.

Exterior colors in the tropics include passionate pastels that
might seem silly on exteriors in cooler climes, but these colors
do work well indoors, anywhere.

Colors fresh from the garden work beautifully indoors. Use
fruits and vegetables as inspiration for color schemes that say
country in a new sunny way.

Kitchen areas without windows depend on color to imply mood-lifting light and sunshine.

When the color scheme is as classically simple as Jack Fhillips's white, sky blue, and khaki, texture is even more important. Here, the lattice-look console plays against the carved and gilded picture frame, nubby upholstery, paper lamp shade, and painted stair balusters.

Simple color schemes are restful. Contrast—like placing the
dark clock and sofa against a very light wall—keeps them
interesting and ultimately satisfying.

Sprightly patterns in lively colors contrasted with a light background create a sense of fun and frolic that gives a traditional living room a holiday air.

Fancy carved furniture moves into sun country with a coat of
blinding white paint that gives it the look of country lace
silhouetted against verdant garden greens. The porch room
offers shade and a shield from the tropical sun.

Pristine white background, furniture, and furnishings look
crisp and cool but are warmed by the high textural contrast of
a wooden ceiling, stuccoed fireplace, and bamboo posts for
the bed.

ROOM
BY
ROOM

iving is casual in the country; it is life carefree. Interiors are treated differently there. Materials must stand up to the wear and tear of exuberant country-goers on perpetual holiday. Furniture finishes and fading should never be reasons to fret. All the comforts, conveniences, and rays of sun count.

A monochromatic scheme is made more dramatic by the play of light and shadow that occurs with latticed shutters at the window.

ENTRYWAYS ❧ In sun-country style, entryways differ architecturally. Whenever possible, entries are made deliberately mysterious to heighten what architects call the ritual of arrival, a sense of having arrived at a very different and therefore wonderful place.

Finding these special entries is not meant to be quick and easy. In a Vermont country house, architect James Strasman places the entry below the bridge, the most visible part of the house, creating a game of hide-and-seek that makes getting there half the fun. Inside the entry—a combination cave and art gallery—an exciting winding stair leads upward. At the top, the bridge is rediscovered, its secret revealed: It is a light-filled, glass-walled living room with forever views of surrounding meadows. The unexpected entry makes arriving in the house and the living room a dramatic event.

At a house in Mexico, the entryway is hidden behind gently descending terraces and winding sheltering walls. The architect's manipulation of sizes, shapes, and directions affects the sense of passage, masking actual time and distance—the outside world seems instantly remote.

Even in modest homes in suburban settings, entries are made more mysterious and sequestered by approaches along circuitous paths that wind in and around trees, past shrubbery—concealing plants, gurgling fountains, and beckoning benches. The idea is the same—to make the outside world go away.

Courtyard-style houses create a sense of Eden in urban areas by concealing entryways behind overscaled gates or huge doors that lead into a courtyard with pool or fountain. All these elements—walls, winding paths, huge gates and doors, and pools and fountains—excite the senses and heighten anticipation as one approaches the entry.

Occasionally, relaxed unorthodox architecture makes an even obvious entry hard to find, creating some sense of mystery and slowing arrival. In a California country house, for example, it is hard to know which of eighteen French doors is the front door. In a converted Louisiana dairy barn, doors opening off either side of the entry breezeway (*trouee*) cause the visitor to pause.

In traditional American houses of the countryside, entryways are often preceded by porches. They are not just places for lazing on a summer day, but are there to slow the transition from busy streets and roads to the entryways. In Pass Christian, Louisiana, one home's broad porch provides a stunning view of the Gulf of Mexico and stands between the entry, a sweeping lawn, and a stretch of highway that is a sightseer's paradise. In Nantucket, a jewel-size porch guards Susan Zises Green's house from street and strangers and provides a sheltering welcome for visitors.

Portals to another realm, entryways should offer a transition from the hectic workaday world to the soothing sanctuary of home. Solid wood-doors or ones with glass panes above eye level are best. All-glass doors expose too much too soon, turning arrivers into voyeurs.

Inside, all these entries share the kind of cleaned-up good looks that are the first indicator of sun country's new direction. The purpose is made clear; the entry is not a waiting room nor a place for lingering. It is a passageway, a visual and emotional link to outdoor and indoor spaces. Therefore, attention-getting, tension-building clutter is banished. Even in interiors based on English manor houses, rows of riding boots, croquet mallets, tennis rackets, and other outdoor gear are exiled in favor of sparse, art-gallery-like spaces.

For many lovers of the new country style, the entry is the starting point for weeding out collections. Knickknacks are out. In their place are only a few important decorative accessories, selected especially because of size, subject matter, color, and texture. These few well-chosen pieces may be expensive or inexpensive, because here it is the quality of the mood, not the furnishings, that counts. "The entry sets the stage for what's ahead," says Florida designer Jack Phillips. "Many leave it to last, but it should be the first area to be designed."

The furniture in sun-country entries is noticeably minimal. This emphasizes that the area is not for lingering. Because its real function is as a passageway, its very nature is transient. Designers find it expedient and logical to use one important large-scale piece of furniture—

perhaps an armoire, interesting console, or a handsome table. Occasionally, there is a bench or chair. When an entry in this new style does serve more than one function—sitting, impromptu light dining, and so forth—furnishings are light and understated so as not to change the focus from entry hall as passageway.

In addition, color takes on several important roles in sun-country entries. First, it defines individual style, which can vary from an ethereal mood based on barely there colors of sky and clouds, to an earthy color scheme rooted in the riotous colors of summer fruits and flowers. Second, the entryway color creates a sense of anticipation as one catches quick colorful glimpses of rooms beyond. Think of an entry in complex soft greens giving way to glimpses of bold pineapple living-room walls on one hand, and watermelon-red dining-room walls on the other. At the head of a stairway, there's a glimpse of morning-glory blue walls.

The adventurous take color play a step further, by combining several wild colors—lemon yellow, azure blue, and apple green—in the entry. Bold color play, beginning in there, is unachievable with single-color palettes. Purely monotone color schemes suddenly seem not just safe but old hat and dull by comparison.

Color is used to furnish an entry in which there is little furniture. Designers do this by painting on finishes or using wallpaper murals, stenciling patterns on the wall or floor, laying colorful ceramic or brick tile floors, contrasting architectural elements with walls, and using countless other ways.

Window treatments in entries as well as throughout sun-country-style homes are practical solutions to such basic problems as privacy and light control. Windows are never fussy, overly frilly, or frivolous. Generally, there is no need for the kind of window treatments that call

A small collection of single, meaningful objects, such as this ship model in an updated sea captain's cottage, enlivens an entry wall, establishing the prevailing mood or passion of the house. Avoid extremes of scale: too large overpowers, too small creates clutter.

attention to themselves, because the view is so much more important. In true country fashion, entryway window-treatment beauty lies in delightfully straightforward choices that are direct, honest, and genuine.

Entryway flooring is always practical. Ideally, a natural stone—slate, unpolished granite, limestone, and Italian porfido stone (commonly used for city streets)—makes a perfect surface. Marble is a soft stone and not generally used. When new marble is used, it is tumbled, which gives it a rustic look. Only very old flooring may be polished marble, because its timeworn good looks are more friendly than formal.

Rustic clay tile, sometimes called Mexican tile, is a favorite choice for floors in North and South America, southern Europe, and tropical islands. Colors range from leather-like cordovan to butterscotch and oxblood. Its waxed and polished surface seems simultaneously warm, cool, and comforting.

Patterned ceramic tiles—especially colorful ones in Portuguese, Mexican, and country-French patterns, are another option. Country Floors, a leading source of decorated tiles in the United States, offers more than a half-dozen patterns with solar-power sun face and sunflower patterns.

In North America's sun-country interiors, plank floors may be painted, whitewashed, antiqued, stenciled, bleached, stained, or left natural. A leading choice for floors throughout the house—plank floors—remains a favorite medium for personal expression.

LIVING SPACES ☞ The purely ceremonial living room is a relic of the past. When it comes to formality, the attitude is—Who needs it? Typical of a new outlook on leisure living, new country homes of a leading singing star in Sag Harbor and an art dealer in Italy's Umbrian Hills forego them altogether. In place of the living room, there are great rooms that

To give a country-style room an elegant air, one can begin with rustic
architecture, light colors, and plain, patternless fabrics. Two other tips are
to avoid clutter and opt for wood shutters instead of draperies.

combine several intimate seating areas, a dining area, and
the kitchen.

Whether living spaces are living rooms, great rooms,
family rooms, or dens—or even when a country house has
one of each—dressed up or dressed down, sun-country-
style living spaces are places of comfort and relaxation.
This elemental mood begins with backgrounds—the term
that designers give to walls, floors, and ceilings.

Backgrounds for living include light, bright, warm,
and friendly walls. Plaster and stucco are favorite rich-
but-rustic materials. When the real thing is not available,
faux-painted finishes and even textured wallpapers in

warm Tuscan and Provençal ochres and weathered yellows and golds simulate the look. Occasionally, they are
enriched with frescos and murals that further the
Mediterranean look.

Painted living-room walls include an occasional classic white, especially over beadboard, wood paneling, or
old brick, but vivid color best expresses the new mood.
New complex paint finishes with layers of colors and textures and wallcoverings in boldly colored stripes and
interesting geometric patterns create intriguing surfaces,
perfect backdrops for any sun-country interior.

Floor coverings for living spaces include all those

used natural materials found in entryways, along with wall-to-wall carpeting in rustic country textures and patterns. Sisal and sisal-looks in easy-care synthetic fibers are among the most frequently used floor coverings. Additionally, area rugs come in so many different colors, patterns, and textures that it is easy to add just the right amount of each to a living-room floor. Flat weaves are a favorite because of their infinite variety, affordability, and cleanability. Indian dhurries, kilims, and Navajo rugs are appealing choices. So are area rugs of sisal, coir, and sea grass—once used only on porches and as doormats—now available in interesting patterns and sophisticated weaves, especially for country-style interiors. Hand-painted floorcloths, originally identified with Early American, colonial, and American-country interiors, also come in updated patterns that make them another sun-country-style option. Area rugs over hard flooring soak up sound and add layers of pretty pattern and cozy texture.

Great seating, and plenty of it, is the first priority for living spaces. The second is arranging seating for cozy intimate conversation, shared television-watching, reading, and listening to music. There is a definite trend toward using more than one sofa in the same room. In this casual style, the two sofas generally do not match, but mix. Even new sofas look inherited, discovered at an estate sale or auction, found, or moved from some previous home.

Fabrics for seating are always practical and easy to clean. An assortment of colors, patterns, and textures avoids the just-purchased look. Brand new and store bought are not casual enough for this laid-back look. Depending on personal taste, sofa covers may be neutral and accessorized with brightly colored and patterned toss pillows. Sofa fabrics, such as Colefax and Fowler English chintzes, French toiles, Victorian florals, quilted

Floor-to-ceiling windows transform a passageway into a garden walk. Milling Road's alluring painted-white chair tempts one to linger.

Souleiado calicoes, carnival stripes, windowpane checks and overscaled plaids, may instead provide the pattern around which a decorating scheme pivots. Pattern mix is important in the country living room. Designers routinely use a minimum of three and as many as seven or more. Pattern scale ranges from a mini-print to a large-scale floral, plaid, or stripe.

Slipcovers—loose or fitted—are common. Certain manufacturers even offer them as an option or addition at time of purchase. Homeowners find that it is a good idea to have one or two pairs made up for switching in and out with a change of season or mood.

Each of two sofas used in a room are often surrounded by lounge chairs. This creates two or more distinctly separate seating groups. One faces the fireplace, the other the outdoors. Occasionally, instead of a second sofa, there is an interesting restful chaise.

One general rule applies for mixing furniture—wooden tables, chests, consoles, armoires, cupboards, and other pieces of furniture should mix well but not match. These highly individual living rooms look as though pieces have been gathered together over generations, or, at least, as though they were chosen with loving care from many interesting sources. Suites of furniture are out. So are country clichés, including manufactured and matching American-country suites of furniture with or without louvers, other oft-repeated motifs, all-white wicker groups, painted furniture with identical repeated motifs, prepackaged French Provençal, and typically tropical groups. They all belong to a best-forgotten past.

For those who love a slightly more exotic look but are not crazy about adding on many frequent-flier miles, globe-trotting buyers and dealers make it easy to select from the world's treasures. Easily available are pieces of old wooden country furniture and authentic reproductions from Europe, India, and the Far East, as well as antique and reproduction country pieces from Mexico. Interesting accent pieces include wrought-iron and stone-mosaic tables, chairs, beds, and consoles from the Philippines. An occasional fancy, formal, or modern piece will also mix well. It is the mix that adds authenticity, texture, and an interesting dimension to sun-country style.

After the sun goes down, sun-country living calls for welcoming interiors made mellow by natural woods, gold-framed pictures, generous splashes of colorful accents, glowing lamps, and in some parts of the world, a working or faux fireplace!

DINING ROOMS
ờ Perhaps the most desirable element in any dining place is a big window with a spectacular view. Next comes a delightful background of cheerfully decorated walls, floor, and ceiling, and then, a generous table and extraordinarily comfortable chairs— the real keys to successful dining anywhere. As for additional furniture, this style, like all other dining rooms, calls for only a few pieces: perhaps a china cabinet for storing dinnerware and a sideboard for serving.

Today's country-style dining room is a perfect place for furnishing à la carte—mixing furniture from various styles, periods, and places—something that homeowners have been doing for centuries. Here is the opportunity to mix . . . a contemporary iron-and-glass

Find beauty in the acceptance of things as they are; don't hide or cover up the elements of life. Designer Jack Fhillips shows in his Palm Beach cottage that open shelving is both practical and beautiful so long as items have been chosen lovingly and used well.

table with rustic wood chairs, a painted table with folding metal garden chairs, a plain peasant's table with sophisticated chairs, or a mosaic-tiled table with wrought-iron chairs. Bringing an outdoor table indoors is a favorite ploy. So is leaving an old wooden table out-of-doors to age to just the right state of ruin before hauling it back into the dining room. The clearest guideline for furnishing the sun-country-style dining room, it seems, is

to express personal style. Each must be true to his or her own muse.

When it comes to wall treatments for the dining room, almost anything goes as long as the look is more country than town. Some borrow from past country styles. The Mediterranean approach begins with plastered or stucco walls covered in ruined or distressed ochre or golden yellow paint. A French Provençal look includes plastered walls imbedded with real straw or plain walls covered in Souleiado-patterned wallpapers. The English look is created with chintz-patterned papers. What brings these typecast treatments out of their traditional country characters and into sun-country-style roles is the new unconventional pairing of wall treatments with unexpected furniture and accessories.

More contemporary country walls sport wallpapers in hot new colors and often incorporate textures that look like hand-painted surfaces. The newest looks like canvas but is actually vinyl, and frescoes are coated in layers of color. Some look aged and timeworn—a cherished traditional country texture. Patterns are broad awning stripes in monotone or contrasting colors, with or without a random overlay of impressionistic arabesques. True chameleons, these papers blend beautifully with all furniture styles.

Although anything goes with wall treatments, dining-room floors tend to be made from materials that require little care and maintenance as long as they add to the rustic charms of sun-country style. Any hard surface, including natural stone and terrazzo, brick, ceramic tile, wood planks, and parquet, may be found in the dining rooms, where area rugs soften the look and soak up sound. Some designers incorporate flat-weave industrial carpeting in textures and colors that create interesting, harmonious

Even traditional decors in serious dark woods can have their hearts lifted sun-country style by removing fussy tablecloths to see how candlelight gleams on polished wood. A loose gathering of field flowers in a simple container is preferable to a formal arrangement in silver or crystal, and cutlery is toned down by using low-luster patinated metal instead of bright silver.

Coir and sisal matting are typical sun-country floor coverings
in areas of the world with a British past. This ideal flooring
marries equally well with painted and natural wood furniture.

backgrounds. Understandably, crumb-hiding natural sisal and other grass floor coverings are not wise choices in dining rooms.

For lighting dining areas, nothing is more wonderful during the daytime than a gentle flood of natural light. Simple blinds, shades, or shutters are favorite methods for controlling glare, especially when the dining room receives late-afternoon sun.

On the other hand, for evening light, a chandelier over the dining-room table is a wonderful touch. Almost any style goes in sun country. Even a fancy crystal chandelier can be wittily at home. For the purist, there are authentic country reproductions galore. It is possible to have a chandelier with a regional flavor (designer Rita Kissner's Big Sky antler chandelier is an example) or a custom-made personal design.

Chandeliers shed a lovely glow over an evening meal, especially when there is a dimmer switch. When less light is needed, candles in glass hurricane globes cast a beautiful romantic light reminiscent of fireflies. What could be more country? Glass hurricane globes are available in hand-blown glass from Mexico and Italy, glass mosaic, and decorated and plain clear glass.

Pretty faience, or French earthenware, loses its city ways and takes on country charm when matched with heavy white lace and fresh flowers from the garden.

Once the floor and wall coverings as well as the lighting have been established, the process of table setting can begin. Setting a table has never been more fun because of the myriad dinnerware designs in a rainbow of colors. There are traditional boldly patterned pottery and handblown glassware from Mexico, Italy, Portugal, and France. There is fascinating dinnerware from France, made of porcelain, a material traditionally reserved for fine, formal china. Harder than pottery or earthenware, it chips less easily, and, because it is vitreous (glass-like), it is less likely to stain. Without elegant gold or platinum trim, it is also dishwasher-safe. Designs deliberately mix and match.

A more important trend is to mix widely available porcelain dinnerware with compatible, original sculptured stoneware and earthenware platters and teapots, ingeniously designed and handcrafted. Artists such as Santa Fe's Mariana Gasteyer intend that their art be enjoyed as it is being used. The big mix at table combines pottery with art ceramic ware, antique silver or pewter flat- and hollowware, handblown ethnic glassware and woven basket ware, naively woven textiles for place mats or a tablecloth, Moroccan and Indian brass or copper accessories. Using handwoven baskets as a container for a centerpiece or in lieu of charger plates is a fresh table-setting idea.

It is easy to see that there is an endless menu of diningroom design possibilities. The great Impressionist artist Monet's dining room at Giverny had an inventive bright yellow-and-blue color scheme with dinner plates to match. It sparked the sun-country style and helped rekindle an all-but-lost love of bright beautiful colors . . . used together.

In sun-country style, there are no rights or wrongs, only a few common objectives— loads of natural light, lots of lively color, and great creature comfort. Good, better, and best choices are decided by the homeowner and the house. Together, they determine the degree of dressiness (forget formality), the most pleasing color scheme, and the furnishings and finishing touches.

BEDROOMS   "To sleep, perchance to dream . . . ," as Shakespeare puts it, is what sun-country bedrooms are about. The trend is to keep this space, like the rest of the house, light and airy. Colors may be sweet, but fabrics must be tailored, never smothered in ruffles.

In this highly eclectic style, furniture does not match. The bed need not match the chest, dresser, night tables, or other furniture in the room. In a romantic California bedroom, for example, there's an iron four-poster with peeling white paint, antique blue-and-white

A glassed-in sunporch with exterior clapboard intact makes an ideal bathroom for a country cottage. Pristine white walls and footed tub are warmed by a wooden storage cabinet and curtainless windows that keep summer green trees in plain sight.

painted chest, cloth-covered round night table, white wicker lounge chairs, and a low Indonesian teak chest. Across the continent in a New York City penthouse done up with sun-country panache, an iron bed enameled black with gilt trim is flanked by small nightstands in white enamel. Across the room, an old wooden blanket chest serves as a coffee table. The sofa, covered in blue-and-white pillow-ticking stripes, is flanked on one side by a mahogany piecrust table and on the other by a wooden standing lamp enameled white to match the nightstands. It is easy to see the same diversity occurring in furnishings throughout the house, but it is especially welcome in the bedroom, the most relaxed room in any home.

In the sun-country bedroom, the bed takes center stage. It may be any style so long as it is not too fine, too fancy, or too formal. Some decorators use a simple Hollywood-style bed with only a stack of plump pillows for a headboard. Other styles include whimsically decorated cottage-style beds, short or tall iron bedposts, tall four-

posters, and tester beds in wood or metal. Occasionally, a bedroom features a mattress laid on a simple wooden base built by a local carpenter. These may be freestanding or occupy a floor-saving niche.

When it comes to bed design, designers and home-owners are taking full advantage of the myriad opportunities for expressing real individualism and true creativity. For example, instead of the more usual fabric inserts, the designer of a house in Mexico ingeniously inserted large photographs of antique oil paintings in the head- and footboards of twin iron beds. A more familiar tactic is to slipcover or upholster a simple headboard in a charming country-style fabric. The headboard may or may not match bed hangings or window draperies.

In southern climes, it is customary to drape the bed with simple mosquito netting, lace, or muslin—a charming, romantic custom that persists even where mosquitoes are not a threat. In chillier locales, coziness is achieved with a tailored canopy of calico, white duck, or patterned chintz.

A modern approach for late-sleepers who love bare windows is to rely on opaque bed hangings to shut out the sun.

When it comes to country bedding, it is chosen first for comfort. Natural fibers—cotton and linen—are obvious choices because they feel good to the touch and absorb perspiration. This keeps the body cooler and is especially important in tropical climates.

As for colors and patterns for bedding, choices from around the world make dressing the bed either a very simple matter or an extremely difficult choice. Crisp white sheets topped with a white lace bedspread or cotton coverlet are the epitome of comfort and chic to many. Others prefer just a wisp of color and choose the barely there pastels. Those with stronger tastes opt for passionate pastels. Traditionalists stick to blue-and-white stripes, English florals, or French Indies patterns. But if none of these choices appeals, the mix-and-match approach borrows sheets from here, pillowcases from there, and a coverlet or quilt from yet another place.

Quilts, an American-country staple, are equally at home in sun country. Especially fitting are nineteenth- and twentieth-century Amish quilts. With their broad areas of striking colors, they look surprisingly modern. Even more contemporary are quilts in colors that reflect the new love of lighter, brighter, almost-liquid colors inspired by sky and water. In addition to American patchwork quilts in new and old patchwork patterns, there are French Provençal *boutis* that feature intricate needlework quilting stitches over fabric in a single pattern and Italian trapunto designs.

Even in sun country, not all days are sunny and some evenings are chilly, so throws are important as light coverups for ritual afternoon naps or the proverbial forty winks. Throws might be found anywhere—on the living-room sofa, in the bedroom, on the porch, and in hammocks—in thoroughly practical wool or linen or in exotic cashmere or silk (a touch of luxury is allowed). Quilted, crocheted, knitted, or woven throws add their comforting touch.

Comfort, increasingly important in decorating styles, is a design priority throughout the home. It is especially vital in the bedroom. Here, thoughtful planning counts—control switches for task and ambient lighting, night tables for handy storage for things needed in bed—a clock, book, pen, notebook, tissue, a carafe for a nighttime drink of water. Something—a table or magazine rack—could hold nighttime reading. Little bedside throw rugs—Oriental, hand-hooked, rag, crocheted, or needlepointed—provide soft landing and well-deserved pampering for feet.

A natural place for fanciful design is the bath, the most private place in the home. New decorated sinks, like this one with its checkerboard pattern, encourage statement-making.

BATHROOMS ❧ Of course, function comes first. But, country baths—especially those in sun country—seem to be anything, as long as they're not too contemporary looking. That leaves enormous leeway in choosing country-style faucets, fixtures, and furnishings. The remodeling magazine editor who asked derisively, "Just how many ways are there in which to deliver water?" had not looked at faucets in a very long time. Country designers and homeowners have—and they have discovered an extraordinary number of different styles and finishes of high-tech faucets, all with special country-style vintage looks.

Pedestal-style sinks, especially those with landing space for toiletries, are a favorite. Sinks for mounting into a countertop come in an astonishing number of different sizes, shapes, and new, lighter, gentler plain colors. Barbara Schirmeister's new colors for American Standard are an excellent example: "Linen" is a softened white, "Day Dream" is barely blue, and "Spring" only hints at green. They are meant to suggest a trickle of fresh clear water. Decorated sinks boast country motifs ranging from silhouettes of birds to pastoral scenes.

New cabinetry comes in an array of styles and in both natural wood and painted finishes. Often, a homeowner discovers an exciting chest or antique dresser in which a sink can be fitted. Countertop materials include delightful decorative tiles, real and faux stone, colorful laminates, colored concrete, and hand-laid natural stone mosaic.

One important point is that country baths sacrifice nothing in favor of quaintness. In fact, quaint is out. An almost Puritan- or Shaker-like simplicity appears in many

Children deserve cheerful rooms in playful places that encourage imagination. This dormered room fills the bill.

old North American houses where the bathroom has been updated or a bedroom converted to master-bath use. That same design approach works in some new structures that respect traditional. The bathroom in an Alabama lake house built by McAlpine-Tankersley, Montgomery architects, looks for all the world like an old-fashioned sleeping porch. The look is underscored by a wood-plank floor and exposed ceiling beams. Banked casement windows and wide white horizontal planks surrounding a gleaming white, freestanding oval tub reinforce the notion of porch. Of course, the tub isn't grandmother's old cast-iron claw foot. In other parts of the country and the world, a more Mediterranean look, gained largely from the lavish use of decorative ceramic tiles, influences country bathrooms.

What all new sun-country-style bathrooms have in common is the integration of interior design with nature, the world just outside the bath. Design welcomes the healing balm of nature into the bath. Whenever possible, this begins with the architecture that allows natural light to flood the room. Overhead are sky windows and sky-lights. Walls are often opaque glass block that let in light but keep out prying eyes. Clear-glass sliding doors let in light and open onto outdoor spaces. When architecture fails to provide these things, designers tend to rely on the magic of mirrors to substitute for light and view.

CHILDREN'S ROOMS ❀

In many decorating styles, children's rooms get just about as much attention as servants' quarters. That is not true in sun country, where children's rooms are every bit as important as those planned for adults. Children's rooms are planned with the same thoughtful considerations for comfort, convenience, and safety. They are designed with the same sure simplicity. There are no theme rooms. When the real thing is present—real sun, sky, and water—reality is far better than any fantasy. When it is not, designers create the effect and the mood with a sunny color palette and simple country style.

ELECTRONIC HAVENS ❀ Home Offices and Media Rooms

❀ More and more people are working from their home offices, so it is not a surprise to find them in sun-country interiors around the globe. Long ago, the trend began to decorate corporate offices as though they were residences. Understandably, real residential offices are decorated in very personal styles. Still, all sun-country home offices do have several things in common. First, the look is relaxed, colorful, contemporary country. There is no hint of the cute or quaint and no attempt to re-create the past—only to perpetuate the life of useful things, such as classic country furniture that serves contemporary needs. Simple peasant tables come to mind. They make ideal desks and conference and worktables. At the same time, they provide a sense of the past and continuity with the future. Rocking chairs with comfortable cushions add a touch of country comfort in home offices just as they did in President John F. Kennedy's Oval Office. Simple Shaker or Windsor chairs are classics that mix well with furniture from other eras. They are also at home with per-sonal computers and halogen lamp fixtures.

Antique country armoires and cabinets to hold tele-vision and video equipment are as much at home in home offices as they are in media and other rooms. They are available in a variety of finishes, including natural wood and decorative painted finishes. Many reproduction pieces come ready to receive modern electronic equip-ment. Holes for wires and wire-management attachments are supplied. Figuring out just what electronic equipment

one wants and where it should be placed may pose a chal-lenge, but decorating these high-tech places in a country style does not.

KITCHENS ❀

Apricot, peach, apple green, musk melon, watermelon, banana, celery . . . they sound good enough to eat, don't they? And so they are, but they're not just names of luscious fruits and vege-tables. These are the colors of sun-country kitchen walls, cabinets, appliances, furniture, and dishes. All country kitchens are the heart of the home, but color sets sun-country kitchens apart. Forget the classic country-kitchen formula—that is, wood paneled walls, dark and heavy beamed ceilings, wood floors. Bright and breezy kitchens are where cooking becomes a friends-and-family adventure and an everyday dinner becomes an event.

Kitchen cabinets set the design direction for kitchens. Increasingly, wherever a kitchen needs a strong dose of good cheer, colorful cabinetry is just what the doctor ordered. New cabinets in painted finishes are available from many sources, but paint gives old wood cabinets a quick, easy, and inexpensive face-lift. In one country kitchen, a coat of cranberry-red paint transformed ply-wood cabinets from ugly ducklings to swans. In another, antiquing old cabinets a soft yellow was like pouring on instant sunshine. Wedgwood-blue paint rescued still another. Painting old wood cabinets pure white is smart; painting the inside of white cabinets watermelon red is sheer genius. It makes opening those cabinet doors a mouthwatering experience. Kitchen owners who continue to love the look of wood find other ways to bring color into these workplaces, such as displaying Fiesta Ware dishes or loading a door-less cabinet with a colorful collection of glassware or china.

Almost as important as the cabinets, the decorated ceramic tiles used as countertops, backsplashes, and wall and floor coverings add both color and pattern to kitchens. Long popular in South American and Medter-ranean kitchens, they have found their way into North American kitchens, where their sunny accents are very welcome.

Laminates in a rainbow of wild and wonderful colors offer abundant options for countertops. They are so readily available, all that's needed to dip into this designer's great grab bag is courage and a strong desire to wake up every morning to the blessing of color. There is no need for constraint. Why use only one when two or three or four marvelous colors are better?

Many interesting attributes are featured in sun-coun-try kitchens. For example, unfitted cabinets and furniture

This recipe for a tasteful kitchen calls for white cabinets spiced with a big dollop of color that comes from a swag topping twin windows and a row of decorative plates. Open shelves are neatly arranged with useful items that take on the role of accessories.

were introduced by Smallbone, an English manufacturer; these cabinets reintroduced the idea of kitchen storage as furniture. A big hit, they have done a great deal to rid the world of the kitchen as laboratory look and reinstate the country-kitchen concept. While Smallbone continues to make unfitted cabinetry, homeowners scour flea markets, estate and garage sales, country auctions, and relatives' attics for dressers, cupboards, armoires, chests, wall-hung shelves, and other instant unfitted pieces to fit into their kitchens, to add new country charm to their kitchens. Old or newly distressed paint finishes add sun-country charm.

In addition, not all appliances come in white, almond, and black. For the color courageous, Aga makes stoves in fire-engine red, yellow, and blue that fit very naturally into sun-country surroundings. Architectural interest: exhaust fans, cooktops, ovens, and grills built into stucco or brick surrounds that look like massive fireplaces are some of the architectural details that add impact in new kitchens with Old Country references.

Unlike most traditional country kitchens, one need not carry a hatchet when visiting sun country; there's no need to chop through forests of hanging herbs. The light and airy look leaves no room for clutter, so it is all gone. A new respect for efficiency, practicality, and reality is present in sun-country kitchens, designed to work well and sensibly. They are not theme kitchens; they are the real McCoy.

OUTDOOR KITCHENS ❧ Many countries allow outdoor dining all or most of the year. Fewer allow outdoor kitchens, but wherever weather permits, they are the quintessential sun-country kitchen. Transplanted Frenchman Michael Benasra, head of Guess Home Collection, created an outdoor kitchen in his southern California home where this talented amateur chef could cook for family and friends. All the furnishings—clay tile floor, painted cabinets, and rustic farm dining table and chairs—remind him of his birthplace in southern France. The tile floor helps keep the kitchen cool. When it gets wet (the kitchen is completely exposed to the elements on the south side), it dries quickly in the open air.

OUTDOOR LIVING ❧ Sunrooms, Garden Rooms, Conservatories, Porches, Loggias, Decks, Patios, Terraces, and Gazebos ❧ Some people would live outdoors forever if only they had the same conveniences that are found indoors. They want to eke out every drop of sunlight, extend the day and even the season comfortably. Because there are so many people who want it both ways, a great deal has been done to devise sunny spaces that combine the best of both indoor and outdoor worlds. These include sunrooms, garden rooms (rooms with one or more walls of windows, under the same roof as the rest of the house), and conservatories (attached to the house on one or more sides but with their own roofs, or freestanding like original conservatories that were created for gardening). All of these areas are fully enclosed, shielding occupants from the elements. Amazing glass technology means that the newest versions

Amdega's summerhouse—a small freestanding building that's partly gazebo, partly conservatory, but totally dedicated to the enjoyment of nature—makes a delightful spot for enjoying refreshments al fresco.

protect from blinding sun, blazing heat, and chilling cold. They may be furnished like any other room in the house and used year-round—and of course they are.

Decorating what essentially is a glass room is a bit different from decorating other rooms. White—possible in other places—is not a good choice for a glass room. It is extremely stark, creates intense glare, and does not weather well. For this reason, designers look to softer pastels, grays, greens, or blues in glare-absorbing matte finishes as background colors for walls.

Flooring, like that in an entry or any hard-wear area, is usually a rustic stone (honed and nonslip), nonskid ceramic tile, brick, concrete, or other easy-to-maintain surface. Occasionally, construction allows wood plank for flooring. Designers avoid this when the garden room actually does have many plants that must be watered and cared for. Flat-weave area rugs add interest to the floor and define various areas of activity. They are also relatively inexpensive, available in infinite colors and patterns, and easy to remove for cleaning.

Upholstery may be used in these rooms, but fabrics must be chosen with care because of fading. This is true even when there are shades (a necessity) and even if they are automatic (electronically controlled), because they're only used some of the time. In enclosed spaces like these, fabrics are not exposed to moisture so they need not be waterproof.

Furniture may be anything that sunlight will not affect too adversely. Traditionally, wicker, rattan, and cane are favorites. They are inexpensive, readily available in a wide assortment of styles, lightweight and easy to move about. So are painted wood, wrought iron, and aluminum—well cushioned, of course.

With only a rustic floor, roof, and a wall or two to shield porches and loggias from the elements, they put users even closer to the great outdoors. Though they may be used for relatively short periods of time in many places, designers and homeowners furnish them with gusto. Wipe-clean, moisture-proof fabrics make it possible to

Michele Benasra's outdoor California kitchen gets the full decorated treatment. Forget about redwood picnic tables. Follow the example of Benasra, designer and head of Guess Home Collection, who opted for vividly colored wipe-clean furnishings that coexist happily with sun, wind, and rain.

place well-cushioned and sometimes fully upholstered pieces on a porch or loggia. Easy-to-clean, inexpensive cotton or flat-weave area rugs add to the sense of room. Plants, easier to care for in this situation, are a natural link to gardens just beyond, and lighting in the form of electric lights, oil lamps, or candles (with hurricane globes to protect from winds) extends the life of the porch long after the sun has set, making it a great place for an evening meal or quiet conversation. Draperies of awning material, heavy duck, and even wash-and-wear designer sheets that can be drawn against sudden summer showers or chilly breezes also extend porch and loggia living.

Porches, loggias, and terraces are strictly fair-weather friends. But when weather permits, there's no better place for soaking up rays of a just-right sun. To comfortable

seating and a table for alfresco meals, one can add an umbrella for protection from a too-hot sun or take a tip from a designer who simply strings up large flags or sheets, hammock-like, between trees as impromptu shade. When there's a need for color, one can add brightly colored pillows and tie colorful banners to trees and shrubs.

Gazebos—tiny little houses with latticed walls—are truly magic places. Tucked away in a corner of the garden or hidden in a patch of woods only a short walk from the main house, they are perfect places for reading a good book or writing a letter to a friend. Built on a promontory with a view of valley, lake, or sea, they're an ideal perch. Most have built-in benches, so decorating them is ever so minimal . . . a cushion for inside; for outside, perhaps a banner or flag of welcome.

The kitchen in the Bridge House, designed by architect James
Strasman, focuses on delight in and full enjoyment of nature
as viewed from safe sheltering confines.

A bold checkerboard floor, large-scaled floral chair covers, and robust country table create an island of interest in this sparkling kitchen cum dining room.

Blurring the line between outdoor and indoor is important in sun country. Here, the coffee table would look equally at home on the adjoining terrace as it does in the relaxed living room.

An elegant mirror and copper tub with antique fittings become the stylish focal point of this bathroom in an old farmhouse.

Designer Mary Douglas Drysdale dresses up a period Pennsylvania farmhouse bedroom in sunflower-bright yellow-checked bed hangings and crewel coverlet.

Architect James Strasman chose stone for walls and floors
that tie this bath to the countryside, visible through slender
windows left elegantly undressed.

A tub for bathing al fresco on a second-story deck is a bit daring but do-able when shielded by a tall view-blocking hedge and wash-and-wear curtains that surround the tub.

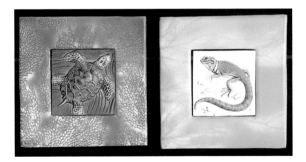

Artists and environmentalists Natalie and Richard Surving, creators of these ceramic tiles, may well have been the first to unabashedly and romatically revel in the unique beauty of creatures not historically considered attractive.

A raised terrace sans walls and windows but replete with a
cushion-covered banquette for sitting and lounging creates a
dining room with unparalleled view.

Souleiado's boldly patterned fabrics enliven lounging chairs that transform a rooftop terrace with expansive views into a summertime living room.

A pergola topped with narrow lathing shields diners from the unrelenting late afternoon sun, while carefully chosen plantings create a cozy natural wall.

A tall plant stand topped with an interesting basket adds a dramatic touch to a cheerful entry.

Milling Road's sofa and chairs shed their skirts for a more open airy look in this sun-dappled living room.

A mosaic tile pattern adds lively interest and regional flavor to this south-of-the-border sun-country bath.

Amdega's mini-conservatory—great for afternoon tea, use as an artist's studio, or children's playhouse— boasts Gothic tracery windows that make for enjoyment of garden views and every ray of sunshine year-round.

Interior designer Rosemari Agonstini's Dallas garden room—a loggia protected from the weather on three sides and overhead—is artfully furnished in a bouquet of floral fabrics for gracious luxurious living.

RUSSIAN HOUSES

RALA

Crystal chandeliers spread sparkling rays of sunshine from curtain-less
windows all around the dining room—even in the country!

In this living room furnished for lounging, a low deep sofa covered in a striking large-scale print takes center stage while pull-up chairs play supporting roles. Overhead, a ceiling fan keeps ocean breezes gently stirring.

Iron tracery twin beds, dressed up for dreaming from head to toe with inserts from photographs of a scenic painting, prove the focal point of this deliciously Spanish-flavored bedroom. Overhead, a ring of mosquito netting suspended from dark beams creates a simple, but romantic backdrop.

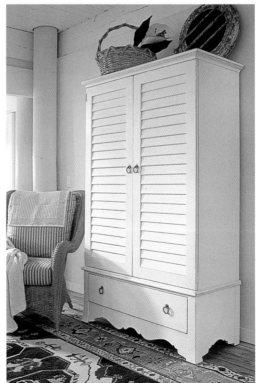

Louvers, an idea borrowed from window shutters, brighten Lexington's handsome armoire and lend a summer-in-the-country flavor to just about any room.

Even when there are no mosquitoes, mosquito netting adds romantic flavor. Here it looks at home above Milling Road's tall colonial-style tester bed, made even more country-looking sans dust ruffle.

Interior designer Mary Douglas Drysdale boldly mixes large-
scale checks, florals, and quilt patterns to call attention to a
delightful niche bed in her Pennsylvania cottage. Wide-plank
floors that deserve to be seen are wisely left bare.

Beautiful ceramic tiles are a traditional Spanish accent that say sun country very clearly in this handsome appealing kitchen. Glass-fronted cabinets show off equally colorful pottery dinnerware.

A well-cushioned exposed wood settee and round table skirted
in a country print back up to an island in the sun in this kitchen
cum great room. Ceramic tile on the floor and below the giant
hood play up the country theme.

A comfortable chair and sturdy table placed behind a media-
room sofa becomes a place to dine, write letters, or study.
Objects on the bookshelves that line one wall add color and
pattern and serve as a strong focal point.

WINDOWS
ON SUN
COUNTRY

In the sun-country style, houses come with windows in all shapes and sizes that provide ringside seats at the greatest show on earth—amazing sound-and-light shows, ranging from sudden storms to clear days on which one can see forever. They call for casual, relaxed window treatments. "The simpler, the better," says designer

Bringing inside simple plank shutters with arched tops originally made for the outside makes great decorating sense. They add to the romantic whimsy begun by pillows and rug from the Tracy Porter Collection for Goodwin Weavers.

The living room in a bridge house by architect James Strasman features an exposed timber ceiling and walls of glass
that tie the house to surrounding nature. Furniture arranged for maximum comfort adds to the relaxed country look.

Jack Fhillip. There are three easygoing window-treatment strategies: bare, barely dressed, and dressed up.

BARE AND BEAUTIFUL ❧ Some windows are architecturally beautiful and deserve to be left bare. Palladian windows (the three-window unit crowned by a half-round window) come to mind. So do tall, slender, elegant French windows and doors like those at colonial Williamsburg with deep, handsomely paneled reveals. Leaving beautiful windows bare is a design-wise practical solution when protection from prying eyes, heat or cold, harmful UV rays, and potential fading are not issues.

What happens when a view is beautiful but the window is not? It's a simple matter to paint the window trim to blend unobtrusively with the wall. The view will star, and the decorating budget will be spared.

Once the sun goes down and the view disappears, even a beautiful bare window can look bleak. One solution is to paint the molding a color that contrasts with that of the walls. The stronger the color contrast, the more powerful the design statement. Another option is to stencil an enriching pattern onto plain molding.

Too-narrow molding can be made to look wider and better proportioned by applying additional molding. If that's not feasible, a simple solution is to paint or stencil a border on the wall alongside and around the molding.

A traditional way to fill a too-empty space between the top of a door and a tall ceiling is with a charming over-the-door panel or plaque. (Ballard, the design catalog, offers several.) The idea works equally well as an over- or under-window treatment Over the window, one can use a panel or plaque like those traditionally used over doors. An ingenious substitution (over doors and windows) is a large porcelain plate or platter, a framed painting or picture, or a graphic painted directly onto the wall. Beneath the window, unbreakable panels or plaques can be added as molding that simulates a panel. Another possibility is to paint a suitable graphic design.

BARELY DRESSED ❧ When a severe window needs softening or a half-blind is needed only part time, then light and lively window dressings are just the ticket. Here are sun-country ways to add just the right amount of function and visual interest when a little dab will do.

SHUTTERS ❧ Houses in southern France are famous for their fanciful and colorful exterior and interior shutters. Shutters also have a long history as favorite window treatments in the United States. A single row of solid or louvered shutters—at window top or bottom—remain an excellent way to block a view or glare. For sun-country interiors, one can antique or paint them a stunning color or treat them to a coat of crisp country white. Shutters in naturally dark-wood colors may seem too heavy, but some wood shutters are available in naturally light woods.

Some of the most interesting shutters are handmade from solid planks with novelty designs cut out or painted onto a painted surface. Although this style is a bit more refined than traditional country style, it still does not demand perfection.

Other shutters come with traditional narrow (one to two inches wide) or more contemporary (two to four inches) wide vanes, or slats. Size and scale are important, especially when the shutter is to be mounted inside the window frame, which must have a deep enough reveal to accept it. Generally, the more narrow the vane, the more refined the look will be—the wider the vane, the more rugged and masculine the look. Stock premade shutters are readily available. Shutters can also be custom-made to fit any window.

CAFÉ CURTAINS ❧ Café curtains hung in a single or double row are a tried-and-true flexible window treatment that are a quick, easy, and inexpensive solution for temporary light control and privacy. They can be hung from brass clips, shirred on a rod,

When they are placed beside beautiful windows, even bathtubs get close to nature in sun country. Here, a tub constructed of decorative tiles is made snug by the arched ceiling overhead.

pleated, or gathered—scallop top and/or bottom or not. Whipped up in textured cottons or in solid or patterned linen, made in opaque or sheer fabrics—the possibilities are endless. Cafés have long been identified with French and American country styles and travel naturally into sun-country interiors.

Wooden cornices and valances make wonderfully crisp toppers for soft café curtains. The wooden surface can be painted or antiqued. For added interest, one can glue on gimp or rickrack, or can stencil or decoupage a design.

BAMBOO BLINDS ❧ Split bamboo blinds—in white, natural woods, tortoise, or colors—are ideal for filtering too-bright light. Originally an islands window treatment, they're at home in sophisticated urban interiors as well as in sun-country rooms worldwide. They can be used alone, with a fabric valance, or behind curtains or draperies. Mounted inside the reveal, they have a sleek finished look. Mounting outside with a reverse roll (the blind rolls toward, not away from, the wall) creates an interesting dimension. However, these see-through blinds don't offer total privacy.

Smith & Noble's Windoware catalog offers dozens of different traditional styles, along with a unique collection of nine different antique colors based on old French blinds from various chateaux, imported from France.

SWAGS, JABOTS, VALANCES, SCARVES, AND TOPPERS ❧ When angular windows need only a bit of softness, texture, and pattern, homeowners might consider one of these tried-and-true solutions. Each calls for only a small amount of fabric deftly applied to the top of a window. They also inspire ingenuity. For example, dinner-size napkins folded and laid across an interesting rod or attached to a wooden pole look and act like a ready-made scarf or topper. Monogrammed plain napkins laid across a wooden pole create a striking, customized valance for any dining room.

BLINDS AND SHADES ❧ An ever-growing number of different kinds of blinds and shades operate on essentially the same principle; they can be lowered for privacy and light control or raised up out of sight and out of mind. Some can be bottom-hung and raised only so high for privacy without blocking a view of the sky. Blinds and shades are an excellent flexible solution and are available in an infinite variety of fabrics, materials, finishes, textures, and colors. Among favorites are the following:

Roman blinds have large flat folds that appear tailored and masculine.

Austrian blinds or *balloon shades* are puffy, curvier, more feminine and romantic.

Horizontal (wide or thin slat) and *vertical blinds* come in wood, metal, and vinyl as well as a host of colors and finishes.

Old-fashioned roller blinds have many virtues that keep them perennial favorites.

Stencilling, painting, appliquéing, and other artful trimming give them newfangled good looks and great sun-country style.

UNCONVENTIONAL SOFT TOUCHES

❧ One should not hesitate to take a leaf from American country's design notebook; after all, there's hardly any new style that doesn't incorporate things from other sources. For example, a barely there grapevine swag or wreath, a valance of baskets nailed directly to the window frame, a wooden cornice, and a painted faux wooden swag are all possibilities so long as one remembers to keep window treatments simple and avoid looking quaint, cute, or fussy.

SUNDAY-BEST DRESSED WINDOWS

❧ Many traditional window treatments can be and are adapted to the sun-country style. Certain designers also prove capable of translating a formal design into something informal and fun. For example, a simple cotton chintz can transform a fussy Austrian shade, usually made up in a fancy silk, into a charming country-style balloon shade. Noted country designer Karin Blake

Individual blinds for each window allow for absolute customized control of too-bright light. Here, a long swag of fabric softens the window lines but can never obstruct the view.

did this for a window in the master bedroom of the "designer farmer" California home she created for actress Candice Bergen, which appeared in *Architectural Digest*.

Simple drapery panels hung from a pole are designers' favorite window treatments wherever there's a desire to quickly and easily close out too-bright sunlight, keep out the chill, or provide privacy for the night. Panels are made of typical country fabrics, including cotton and linen. Whenever fabric is patterned, those patterns are apt to be old country-style favorites, including checks, plaids, stripes, florals, and toiles. Designer Jack Fhillips of Palm Beach chose white cotton duck for his living-room curtains. For interest, he trimmed them in washable raffia. Other favorite trims include flat woven braid and grosgrain ribbon.

Occasionally, a designer adds a soft valance to hide drapery hardware or frame a view. Sometimes, the valance fabric matches the draperies. At other times, it does not. In a bedroom, for example, Fhillips made a curtain valance of recycled nautical flags.

Lace curtains simply shirred on a wooden or iron rod are also favorites. Lace is a centuries-old favorite country fabric, especially when it's coarsely woven and rustic. Interior designer Susan Zises Green chose white lace for curtains for the entryway of her Nantucket cottage because it let the light peek in and her peek out at miles of blue sky. In another example, Karin Blake chose lace curtains for a wall of French windows and doors in Candice Bergen's Beverly Hills master bedroom.

Sheer, light-admitting fabrics such as lightweight muslin is another wonderful country-curtain fabric. Legendary designer and arbiter of taste Else de Wolfe hated lace but loved muslin and used it endlessly for town and country curtains. It's a perennial favorite because it's pretty, practical, and inexpensive.

Sun-country style is one of great freedom in interpretation. There are only two "thou shalt nots": One should not resort to heavy layered looks or use formal fabrics.

Natural rugged materials, such as the random fieldstone that creates this chimney breast and heavy timber overhead, emphasize the country mood in this living room where stacked windows admit light and views.

Setting the bed on an angle means that sleepers can awaken to a better view through the dormer window topped by a novelty valance.

PRACTICAL WINDOW MATTERS

Before deciding on sun-country-style window treatments, consider these practical problems that may point the way to appropriate design solutions:

Providing privacy: Chances are that for houses on tropical islands, such as the St. Lucia house in chapter 2, privacy will never be an issue. Then, window coverings aren't necessary. But whenever privacy is an issue, window coverings must provide it.

Veiling a view: Not all beautiful homes have beautiful views. Ideally, a city apartment in the sun-country style would open onto a delightful penthouse garden terrace. Realistically, it may have windows that open onto the brick wall of a neighboring apartment building. By the same token, not all suburban or even rural views are wonderful from every window. When a view needs to be veiled, a well-designed window treatment can serve as a beautiful disguise. Consider translucent or sheer curtains, blinds that can be partially opened to let in light but shut out the view, or louvered shutters that admit some light and no view.

Controlling glare: It may be necessary to shield a writing desk, reading chair, or computer or television screen from glare. This is probably a temporary situa-

tion, calling for a flexible solution that permits quickly and easily returning to a great view. Consider blinds, shades, or draperies.

Blocking UV rays and fading: UV rays and fading are greater threats in some areas than in others. Some window glass is already treated to a tint that offers protection, but window treatments may also be needed to prevent problems. Hunter Douglas's "Pleated Shade" comes in metallized fabrics that the company says reduces UV rays.

Controlling the climate: In some parts of the world and in homes without properly designed windows, extreme heat and cold call for thermal-lined draperies and other window dressings to help keep rooms more comfortable. Since not all sun-country-style homes are in the South, be realistic and add these aids to livability if they're needed. The right selection of sunny colors and patterns will keep the look without sacrificing function.

Considering the unconventional: One designer closed off a too-cold bay window in an upstate New York kitchen with a wall of recycled French doors that kept the view exposed, the cold out, and the heat in. In the summer, the French doors fold back against side walls and out of the way.

Flanking a garden window with bookcases and building in a window seat below create a perfectly natural place for a nice read or catching a quick forty winks.

Classic symmetry found in interior designer Anthony Catalfaro's pairing of windows and wallhangings adds soothing calm to a bed-sitting-room.

Brightly colored floral bedcovers and draperies play up the natural connection between the indoors and the garden visible through opened French doors

Tropical-country style omits curtains in favor of shutters and French doors open to the terrace. An old-fashioned electric fan stirs tropical breezes.

Light furniture against vivid walls turns the tables on traditional color schemes. Sheer curtains wrap windows in white wisps that filter and soften the sun.

A fascinating white metal bed creates a haven of rest and an exciting focal point in a dormered bedroom gift wrapped in a floral motif. Interior designer Susan Zises Green adds more flowers to the mix with a painted dresser and vivacious country quilt.

Star of this light and lively Philippines-country bedroom is the painted iron bed enlivened with hand-applied stone mosaic from the Sun Country Style collection by Patricia Hart McMillan and Raphael Legacy Designs. Furnishings and accessories are few and bold.

Sheer curtains in exciting colors draw attention to a wall of traditional French doors in a French-country house filled with casually comfortable furniture.

When the view is as breathtaking as this trompe l'oeil scene of the American Southwest, the best window treatment is no treatment at all. The spot is ideal for a dressing table.

LIGHTING
UP THE COUNTRY
NIGHT

After the sun goes down, fireflies need a little help to light up the night. Light moves people. Artists are especially sensitive and notoriously susceptible to its strangely beguiling charms. The Impressionists set up their easels in the fields of Provence. The Hudson River school

Souleiado's charming chintz-patterned textiles are synonymous with French-country style, forerunner of today's sun-country decorating style. Cozy textiles and candles with hurricane globes team up with a classic country chandelier to brighten a dining room.

strove to capture the essence of light in that mountainous region. Georgia O'Keeffe fell under the spell of light near Santa Fe, made her home and built a life and career there.

The quality of light in artists' favorite haunts is extraordinary, but even ordinary light has its charms. Hence, new homes include whole walls of windows and *no-treatment* window treatments that leave every bit of the window exposed. A love of light explains the rush to garden rooms, conservatories, decks, patios, gazebos, and gardens. It also explains the current infatuation with mirrors that reflect light, magnifying its presence to the nth degree. Taking advantage of every speck of sunlight is more than a trend; it is now a way of life reflected in the colors of the paints we choose. Often, it's "sunshine in a can" that we're seeking.

What happens when there is no sunlight, when the day is cloudy and gray and that celestial orb disappears below the horizon? In sun country, home decorators find ingenious ways to light up the night (and gloomy days).

Surprisingly, even bright sunlit rooms need extra artificial illumination. Lighting designers point out the need to balance light in rooms with

What could be more country, more casual than a chair pulled bedside to serve as an auxiliary nightstand?

huge window walls by providing additional illumination in areas away from the windows. A well-illuminated interior must rely on more than a few decorative table or floor lamps. Well-distributed ambient light is a basic requirement. High hats and other ceiling fixtures are acceptable and even desirable in this new but still-practical country style. Granted, these modern fixtures should be discreetly recessed whenever possible and made to appear to blend into the ceiling.

In addition to ceiling-recessed fixtures, in rooms with extremely high ceilings and exposed beams, fixtures may also be mounted on the beams. Lamps aimed both up and down create even, all-over lighting. Bouncing an up-light off the ceiling softens shadows, making the room look larger. It overcomes shadowing by down-lights that make

occupants look tired and older than they actually are.

Occasionally, special kinds of fixtures serving as ambient lights may be called on to overcome specific problems. One lighting designer reportedly relies on high-pressure sodium lights with their yellow glow to light up rooms still paneled in dark woods that soak up light. In addition to creating ambient light, these lamps bring out highlights in dark wood, making it seem brighter and livelier.

In addition to ambient light, accent lights are needed to highlight small areas. Low-voltage spotlights mounted to the ceiling or beams can highlight and accentuate special-interest areas, such as important art works or seating groups, and a focal point, such as a mantel. When these accent lights (or lamps, as they're sometimes called) are adjustable, they can easily be moved so that the angle of the light beam is repositioned. This is a good idea wherever artwork is continually relocated or furniture is regrouped. Further, adding a dimmer switch can be useful if the room converts to a media room. In addition to overall or ambient lighting and accent lights, rooms need task lighting. Table and floor lamps perform this lighting job.

Providing these three different types of lighting is called *layering*. The layering technique allows the greatest flexibility and livability. Of the three different kinds of lighting, portable table and floor lamps offer the most possibilities for personal expression. Choices are numerous. First, one can either buy a brand new lamp or give an old one a new lease on life. Secondly, a particularly creative person may decide to make a lamp or select a suitable unexpected object and have a lamp maker transform it into one.

The quality and creativity of new lamps in the sun-country mode are so astounding it is almost difficult to imagine that anyone would have trouble finding the perfect lighting. Some lamps include enchantingly lifelike ceramic or majolica pumpkin and squash bases. Others are made from ceramic, metal, and wood, sporting sun

Light-colored kitchen cabinetry is a hallmark of sun-country style. It mixes beautifully
with loads of lighting, wooden or ceramic floors, and colorful accessories.

faces, while still others are ceramic lamps with giant cacti bases for those creating a southwestern mood. In addition to these novel lamps, there is a plethora of handsome lamps in diverse materials that will add just the right touch to any decorating scheme.

Old favorites in ceramic, metal, and wood are still very welcome in sun country—with or without a face-lift that includes an interesting new shade. Often, just moving an old lamp to a new place allows it to be seen in a new, more attractive light! The only real guideline—remember, country *encourages* mixing a variety of styles and periods, including contemporary—is that the lamp not be too fancy and that it work well with the overall scheme.

When lamps with meaning are sought, it is a good idea to follow the lead of those who seek out odd and unusual objects and transform them into lamps. Done

with good taste and true wit, this is personal expression at its best. Even though this new country style avoids the too-quaint, it's fun to see ruined watering cans, old ceramic pitchers, interestingly shaped and colored bottles, antique tins replete with advertising art, jugs, urns, candlesticks, pieces of gnarled wood, junk iron, wooden boxes, rusted paint buckets, wooden newel posts, or other architectural fragments crafted into handsome lamps.

Creating lamps from found objects—especially when they are found in one's own attic—is memory making. And memories are a large part of what sun-country style is all about. Those who have done it know that imagination is all it takes, along with the telephone number of that little old lamp maker who knows just how to create memorable, UL-approved lamps from the strangest of things.

Interior designer Jack Fhillips hangs a traditional brass chandelier above
a rustic wooden table in his Palm Beach shipbuilder's cottage. On the
table, candles in hurricanes add to the midsummer's night mood.

Candles on mantel and tabletop stand at the ready to light up
the night in this sunflower-bedecked Florida living room.

CANDLE POWER

When we think of lighting, we inevitably think of electricity. But while electric lights light up our lives, it is candlelight that lights up our hearts. Because it is so soft and gentle, so reminiscent of nurturing firelight, candlelight remains a favorite way to add just enough light to a dining room, garden room, porch, patio, poolside, or wherever people love to linger in the evening. It slows the pace, turns back the clock, and gentles the soul. Candles even seem vaguely akin to the fireflies that flit wildly just beyond their own flickering glow. Indoors, candles are wonderful with or without hurricane globes. On porch and patio, they need protection from the wind.

The variety of candles from which one can choose is staggering. There are fanciful hand-dipped candles that are made by repeatedly dipping the wick into hot wax, building the candle layer upon layer. Rolled candles are made by rolling sheets of wax around a wick. Molded candles, made by pouring melted wax into a mold and allowing them to harden, are less expensive. Sizes range from super thick to small votive candles. Name a color and it is probably available in a candle. Shapes vary from short and chunky to tall, slender, and elegant. Then, there are the novelty candles that look like flowers, vegetables, fruits, toys, sculpture, and so on. Texture provides another dimension and so does a variety of materials—flower petals, beads, and so on—added to the wax. Scent bestows a final and utterly delightful dimension to the pleasure of candles as the ultimate in country-style night light.

Up-light sconces direct light toward the ceiling to create indirect lighting and fewer shadows in this seaside bath. Ceiling fixtures for general illumination should augment task lights such as sconces.

A tall slender candlestick lamp on one side and a floor lamp
that does double duty as both chair and bedside lighting
brighten up this bedroom with its pencil-post bed.

This End Up's red plaid rocker is a showstopper that means to slow down the pace from hectic to easygoing in this gracious country living room.

When the sun goes down, layers of lighting come into play in this kitchen/dining room. Overhead ceiling spots provide overall ambient lighting. The chandelier highlights the dining table. A pair of candlestick lamps accentuate the island while under-cabinet lights brighten up the countertop.

SUN
COUNTRY
ACCENTS

he picnic table on the spanking new deck overlooking a lovely

remote lake desperately needed a centerpiece. "Flowers,"

said the decorating editor of a national magazine. But there

were no flowers, no container, and the nearest florist was

thirty miles away. Driving there and back would mean losing the sun, ruining

Flowers and plants enliven a corner where a round table dressed in a
Souleiado cloth stands ready for refreshments. Beautifully decorated
functional ceramics are also artful accessories

the shoot, and missing the magazine's deadline. A country girl in her past life, the resourceful New York City editor went to a nearby pile of rubbish left by the building crew, pulled out a rusty paint bucket covered in Jackson Pollock–like paint drips, filled it with water and plunked it down on the table. From the field at the edge of the lawn, she pulled an armful of wildflowers—weeds, really—and arranged them in the bucket. "Wow, pretty sophisticated," said the renowned architectural photographer with admiration, and he shot the picture.

To say that many accessories in country-style interiors have an interesting past life is probably an understatement. It's perhaps more accurate to say that most do, although their stories might be more or less colorful than that of the real-life rusty paint bucket. It's obvious that recycling interesting old objects and reassigning them new roles and functions as decorative accessories is a true hallmark of this practical style.

Sun-country style continues this uncommonly sensible practice of finding ingenious uses for ordinary things. Vines are fashioned into wreathes and swags. Artful branches become curtain poles. Old garden gates are transformed into wall art and headboards. Salvaged shutters become standing screens. Weather vanes become mantel sculpture. Small zinc washtubs become magazine holders. Cups, bowls, and pitchers do double duty as vases. Plates, platters, and bowls come down out of cabinets and onto kitchen and dining-room walls. Tiny toys are mounted on painted boards to become interesting art. Outmoded, discarded items that are no longer useful but very attractive—dinner bells, snuffboxes, hand-operated farm tools—become collections and fascinating displays. Framed calendars, photographs from old books, and family photographs enliven hallway walls and enrich homes.

Carefully controlled clutter is the only kind allowed in sun-country interiors, as in this room by designer Jack Fhillips, who masses favorite things in an artful array.

Part of the charm of country accessories is their sense of appropriateness. The objects gathered by designer Jack Fhillips for his Florida country house reflect the facts that the house was built by a sea captain, is near the beach, and is dressed in blue and white—classic nautical colors. Paintings of sailing ships, a clutch of old oars, and brass sea lanterns nicely echo the nautical mood. Designer Rita Kissner discreetly chose a few key accessories to underscore the westerness of the Big Sky house she designed for clients not interested in a purely Montana look. A handsome antler chandelier and an antler mirror were powerful enough to make the western point nicely.

Accessories in sun-country homes tend to be diverse, to have come from many different places. What designers call "the mix" is very much a part of the magic of this global style. It makes room for things that capture the fancy, no matter the provenance. African art, Philippine mosaic boxes, French porcelain, Portuguese ceramic tiles, Italian pottery—here and abroad they're likely to get mixed with more typical indigenous or perhaps American-country collectibles in a way that seems entirely natural and totally unself-conscious.

Are there any new rules for accessorizing in sun-country style? Probably not. The freedom in this style should not be surprising. After all, it reflects the times—a period of the greatest personal freedom perhaps ever in history. But old rules of good taste and basic design still prevail. They have to do with organizing collections in pleasing groups of like or similar objects and complementary scale, texture, and compatible color.

There is, however, a new attitude toward accessories; they should not seem to be mere clutter. The new cleanness and orderliness calls for fewer accessories. It also calls for higher *quality* accessories. The accent on quality does *not* mean that accessories should be more expensive,

There is strength in numbers as any general knows. Here, a plethora of metal candleholders gang up wonderfully atop a simple mantel.

exclusive, or precious. It does mean that they should be more importantly scaled, textured, shaped, and colored.

Many new accessories fill the bill, such as fascinating new lamps in exciting new colors, shapes, and materials; lamp shades found in more intriguing shapes and materials than ever; and new mirrors framed in intertwined oak branches, replete with oak leaves and three-dimensional, life-like acorns—some of the numerous styles that surprise and delight. In addition to new things, other outlets such as estate sales, auctions, tag sales, garage sales, consignment shops, thrift shops, and salvage yards are all great places for scrounging for the old, odd, and offbeat.

Displaying accessories whose only role is to please the eye is done in time-honored ways. Collections are arranged as artfully as possible in glass-fronted cabinets and open shelves or as tablescapes. What's new is that less is more. Sun-country rooms are not smothered by items that cover every inch of available space.

Perhaps because this style is still new and global,

fewer quilts are visible and fewer still are hung on walls. Rooms no longer look like quilt bazaars. Instead, the quilts one is likely to see are carefully selected by color and pattern to enhance a particular room. Quilt collections are more often carefully folded and beautifully stacked behind protective closed doors.

Though baskets are not the stronghold in sun-country style that they are in traditional country style, they are a recognized art form and tend to be displayed singly. Some serve as both an interesting object and magazine holder.

Dried flowers and plants, reminiscent of fall and winter, are not so prevalent in sun-country interiors, which celebrate spring and summer and living, growing things. When they are present, they are likely to be in one large, significant, colorful arrangement. Occasionally, there is a lovely small arrangement, such as dried roses in a child's old pewter cup. It's the dotting of surfaces throughout a room with countless arrangements that's definitely out.

Clocks, important in some styles, do not seem to be

No one does accessories better than Mother Nature. Usually,
she offers flowers but here she displays other fruits of her
labor—branches replete with apples in a lovely vase.

terribly important accessories in sun-country style. Perhaps this is a style that wishes time to stand still. More likely, it is that clocks are built into so many things: radios, television sets, microwave ovens, and stoves. Legendary decorator Elsie de Wolfe dictated that every room have a clock and deplored the fact that Americans were not so inclined. Perhaps if she could see modern appliances with clocks, she'd think better of Americans— but perhaps not, since she loved decorative clocks.

Mantels are important throughout sun country. It's surprising, actually, how chilly even hot desert and tropical places can become after sundown. Then, a lighted fire takes away the chill. Decorating a country mantel means arranging a few appealing objects. Favorite things for mantels are clocks, old oil paintings (framed or unframed, hung or propped), a clutch of candlesticks, a sculpture, a rigged sailing ship, fresh pineapples or Granny Smith apples all in a row, large shells, birds' nests, an intriguing rock, fresh flowers from the garden, a piece of pottery by a child, a timeworn jug, or a found gear from an old tractor. Objects are arranged asymmetrically, which is less formal than symmetrical balance.

Asymmetrical balance in arranging objects on tabletops is also preferable to a formal arrangement. It's a bit more challenging but ultimately more suitable. Asymmetry also encourages change, something that seems natural to country living and to accessorizing, since there are always so many possibilities and so little space.

One strong object is enough to capture and hold the attention. In this case, it's a handsome pitcher atop a plain and simple table.

A glass vase and bowl share the same geometric design but offer diversity of shape and purpose.

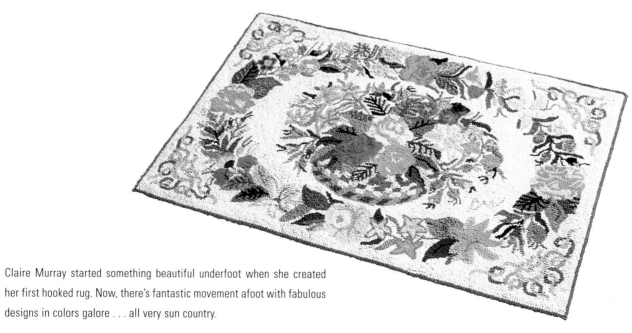

Claire Murray started something beautiful underfoot when she created her first hooked rug. Now, there's fantastic movement afoot with fabulous designs in colors galore . . . all very sun country.

Neatness counts when favorite things that have only their owner in common are massed together. Here, unrelated things coexist happily because each is given its very own space.

What could be more sun country than a lamp with a sun face? This one—a must have—is the creation of Salon du Meuble de Paris.

Birds of a feather flock together—beautifully. Here, wicker-
covered bottles and jugs imply hospitality and conviviality.

Dolls are not just child's play. This collection graces the hallway of a Key West cottage.

Painted furniture, which had its moment then went away, is back. And, it just gets prettier each season. Here, Habersham's tall chest and long table demonstrate just how diverse painted patterns can be.

Sun lovers of southern France found out early that colorful faience, like this by Lunéville, France's oldest faience maker, gives every meal a festive air. Afterwards, it's a visual delight. Display it on open shelves and in cabinets with either glass-fronted doors or no doors at all.

RESOURCES:
A FEW FAVORITES

New and wonderful little shops crop up continuously, often in unexpected places. Here are a few favorite sources for house and garden. Most are readily available no matter where one lives.

BOOKS

Phillips, Betty Lou
*Provençal Interiors: French Country
Style in America*
Gibbs Smith, Publisher
P.O. Box 667
Layton, UT 84041
Ph: 1-800-748-5439
Fx: 1-800-213-3023
Web: www.gibbs-smith.com

Wagoner, Annette, ed.
Furniture Facts
J. Franklin Publishers, Inc.
c/o Selling Retail International
P.O. Box 14057
Tulsa, OK 74159
Ph: 1-800-444-6141

The lighted fire may say "chill," but the sun-ray mirror on the mantel and a bevy of decorated straw hats hanging above the mirror reaffirm a sun-country mood.

Witynski, Karen, and Joe P. Carr
Mexican Country Style
Gibbs Smith, Publisher
P.O. Box 667
Layton, UT 84041
Ph: 1-800-748-5439
Fx: 1-800-213-3023
Web: www.gibbs-smith.com

CATALOGS

American Quilts
Ph: 1-877-531-1619
*Handcrafted American quilts in a wide
array of patterns and colors.*

Ballard Designs
Ph: 1-800-367-2810
*Unique items, classically designed items
for use throughout the house.*

Sunflowers—a country icon—are at home in this sunny American southwestern interior.

This End Up's casual mix of clear and colored glass is very sun country!

Chambers Linens
Ph: 1-800-334-9790
Fine, affordably priced linens in interesting patterns and colors.

Garnet Hill
Ph: 1-800-622-6216
Uniquely designed bedding and other household items.

Gardner's Eden
Ph: 1-800-822-9600
Fresh charming designs for indoor and outdoor use.

Golden Valley Lighting
Ph: 1-800-735-3377
Custom lighting fixtures in designs that seem special.

Gump's Interiors by Mail
Ph: 1-800-248-8677
Captivating designs—many from the Orient—to add a special touch to rooms throughout the house.

Horchow Home
Ph: 1-800-395-5397
Items designed with classic good taste for use throughout the house.

IKEA
Ph: 1-800-225-IKEA
Clean-cut common-sense furnishings made in Scandinavia for use throughout the home.

Janovic Plaza
Ph: 1-800-772-4381
Great source for paints and wallpapers.

Palm trees within and without underscore a sun-country ambiance that embraces Milling Road's traditional dark-wood furniture and cushy upholstery.

Smith & Hawken
Ph: 1-800-776-3336
Ideal source for outdoor furnishings.

Smith & Noble Windoware
Ph: 1-800-248-8888
A storehouse of blinds and shades in a wide range of textures, colors, and styles.

Spiegel
Ph: 1-800-Spiegel
A big catalog and convenient source of well-styled, well-priced furnishings.

Studio Steel Custom Chandeliers
Ph: 1-800-868-7305
Smartly styled custom lighting fixtures.

Sundance
Ph: 1-800-270-6617
Western style to the nth degree that mixes well with sun-country style.

This End Up Furniture Co.
Ph: 1-800-627-5161
Great source for affordably priced, good-looking, simply designed furnishings.

DESIGN CENTERS

(Visit the many country-style showrooms in these design centers with your designer or architect, or use a designer provided by the center itself. Call for an appointment before you go.)

New York Design Center
Ph: 1-800-732-3272

Design Center of the Americas
(DCOTA)
Dania, FL 33483
Ph: 954-920-7997

Designers & Decorators
(D&D) Building
979 - 3rd Avenue
New York, NY 10012

Pacific Design Center
Ph: 1-800-732-7261
Web: www.pacific.com

MAGAZINES

(These favorite magazines are a treasure trove of information and a feast for the eyes.)

Architectural Digest
P.O. Box 59060
Boulder, CO 80323-9060

Much of artist Mariana Roumell-Gasteyer's ceramic pottery is in art galleries and museums, but each of her unique decorative stoneware and earthenware pieces is intended by her to be used—to spread its own sunshine, highlighting and transforming everday moments into special events.

British Country Homes & Interiors
Ph: 011-44-171-261-6895
Fx: 011-44-171-261-6405

Country Home
Ph: 1-800-374-9431

Country Living
Ph: 1-800-888-0128

House Beautiful
Ph: 212-903-5000

Maisons Côte Sud
Newsstands

Southern Accents
Ph: 1-800-882-0183

Veranda
Ph: 404-261-3603

MANUFACTURERS

(These manufacturers make great products and information available. Call for literature and the name and location of their nearest retail representatives.)

DeTonge
Valbonne, France
Ph: 33-93-95-80-00
Wonderful source for authentic antique-style, painted, French-country furniture.

Grange
Ph: 1-800-Grange-1 or
212-685-9057
Leading maker of classic French styles updated for today's lifestyles.

Harden Furniture
8550 Mill Pond Way
McConnellsville, NY 13401-1844
Web: www.harden.com
Well-made furniture without gimmicks, just right for today's country living.

Hickory Chair
Ph: 1-800-349-HKRY
Web: www.hickorychair.com
Handsome furniture for the seriously relaxed home.

Flor Gres's colorful ceramic tile pours sunshine on walls and floor.

Lexington Furniture
Ph: 1-800-LEX-INFO
Web: www.lexington.com
Lexington invented the weekend furniture look and continues to create trend-setting country-style furniture.

Martex
Ph: 1-800-458-3000
Web: www.martex.com
Super bedding for casual but smart living.

Souleiado
Tarascon, France
Fx: 90-91-01-08
Maker of legendary fabric that's synonymous with southern France's sunny decorating style.

Wellborn Paint & Color
Ph: 1-800-228-0883
(or 1-800-432-4067 in NM)
Rich, velvety-looking paint in special colors that astound.

Schreuder Paint
(from Fine Paints of Europe)
Ph: 1-800-332-1556
Extraordinary paint colors available only from this maker. To see is to believe!

This one-of-a-kind handmade quilt by Tessie Ephlin Malone of Texas celebrates sun-country style's new sun-loving pastel color palette. Lightweight and called a "summer quilt," it can be used year-round as a bed cover.

Living in the sun is easy when the fabrics are Souleiado's pretty and practical cottons.

RETAIL STORES

ABC Carpet & Home
New York, NY 10010
Ph: 1-800-458-2414
Everyone's favorite home-furnishings destination in New York City. The flea-market aura and vintage café make shopping an adventure.

Pier I Imports
Ph: 1-800-447-4371
Web: www.pier1.com
A great place for impulse shopping and spontaneous decorating. Furnishings are bright, colorful, dynamic, and sensibly priced.

Pottery Barn
Ph: 1-800-922-9934
Chic, simple furnishings make this the place for good-looking basics for

kitchen. living room, bedroom, and dining room, and for accessories throughout the house.

Roche Bobois
183 Madison Avenue
New York, NY 10016
Ph: 1-800-972-8375
French-made furniture in a variety of styles and periods.

Toujours Provence
(DeTonge and Souleiado)
85 SE 6th Avenue
Delray Beach, FL 33483
Ph: 561-330-0561
Fx: 561-330-0562
This charming little shop is just the place to find painted French furnishings without traveling to Provence. Stay for lunch or snacks at the bistro.

PHOTOGRAPHIC CREDITS ☙

Agostini, Rosemari, Interior Designer (courtesy), 41, 98, 99

Amedga: 12, 16, 98, 104

American China: 77

Armstrong World Industries: 117

The Blachere Group, U.S. representatives of Lunéville Faience: 75, 143

Brantley, Robert (Jack Fhillips, Interior Designer), 30, 31, 60, 61, 69, 72, 82, 124, 126, 134, 140, 143

Brooke, Steven: 76

Budji (courtesy Budji, Inc.), 36, 113

Chesapeake, Hearth & Home Collection: 57

De Tonge Furniture (courtesy Tourjours Provence), 46, 56

Domenech, Carlos: 25, 48, 58, 66, 68, 74, 82, 83, 86, 91, 96, 97, 107, 116, 127, 128, 137, 141, 150

Elitis: 120, 135

Fhillips, Jack (*see* Brantley, Robert)

Fieldstone: 106

Florim Ceramich, Flor Gres "Melange": 148

Frances, Scott: 114

Georgia Pacific: 115

Goodwin Weavers (Sheffield & Galloway's Tracy Porter Collection), 108

Grange (courtesy Salon du Meuble de Paris), 47

Green, Susan Zises, Interior Designer (*see* Roth, Eric)

Habersham: 142

The rocking chair, an American invention at ease even in the White House, is entirely at home on this seaside second-story porch with view.

☙

Hunter Douglas: 112

Kissner, Rita, ASID (*see* Skott, Michael)

Lexington: 102

Milling Road: 71, 95, 103, 146

Mitchell, William B., The Mitchell Group: 32, 33

Nasta, John: 78, 131

Peterson, B.J., Interior Designer: 101

Raphael Legacy Design (*see* Tan, Bernard)

Rosemary Beach: 50

Roth, Eric (Susan Zises Green, Interior Designer), 6, 10, 28, 29, 40, 42, 95, 118, 144

Roumell-Gasteyer, Mariana: 143

Rutt Custom Cabinetry, Kitchen Solutions, Bronx, NY: 60

Rutt Custom Cabinetry, Baker Woodcraft, Flanders, NJ: 126

Salon de Meuble de Paris: 139 (courtesy Francois Chatain)

Samuelson, Jeremy (courtesy Guess Home Collection), 34, 81

San Ysidro Ranch: 22, 23

Shelburne, Garden Walk Collection: 52, 55,

Skott, Michael (Rita Kissner, ASID, Interior Designer), 42, 43

Souleiado (courtesy Tourjours Provence), 44, 93, 122, 132, 133, 149 (top and bottom)

Strasman, James, AIA: 83, 88,106

Surving Studios: 4

Tan, Bernard (Joselito Dorotheo, Interior Design; courtesy Raphael Legacy Design), 19, 119

This End Up: 51, 53, 63, 84, 87, 130, 138, 148

Vierra, Steve: 18, 54, 57, 84, 65, 113, 116, 129

Vitale, Peter: 39, 45, 59, 70, 73, 88, 89, 92, 93, 94, 100, 101, 102, 104, 105, 111, 120, 121, 136, 139, 147

Von Einsiedel, Andreas: 26, 37, 38, 64, 65

Vorillon, Dominique: 21, 24

Watkins, Larry: 20

Winterthur (Claire Murray Rug): 138